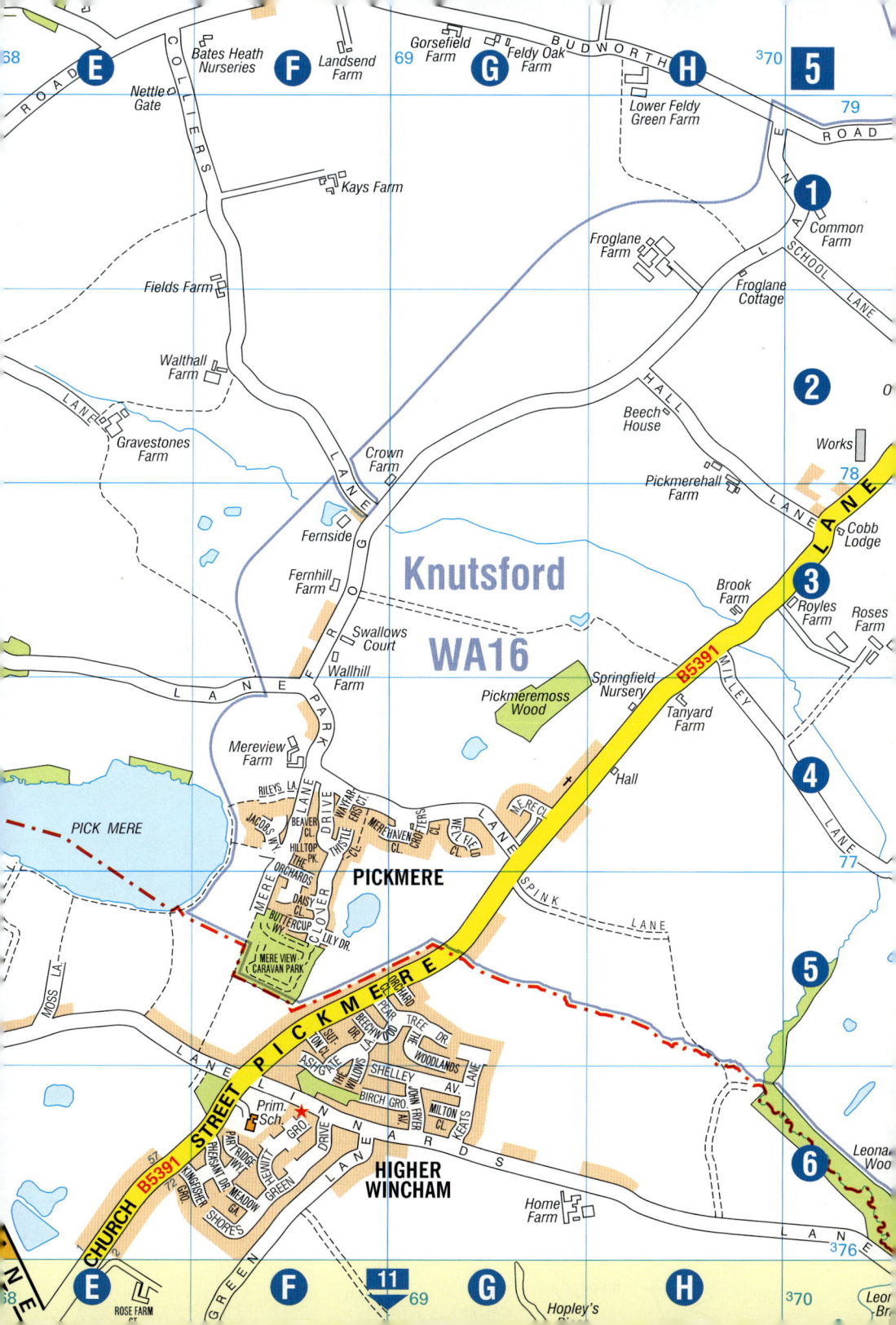

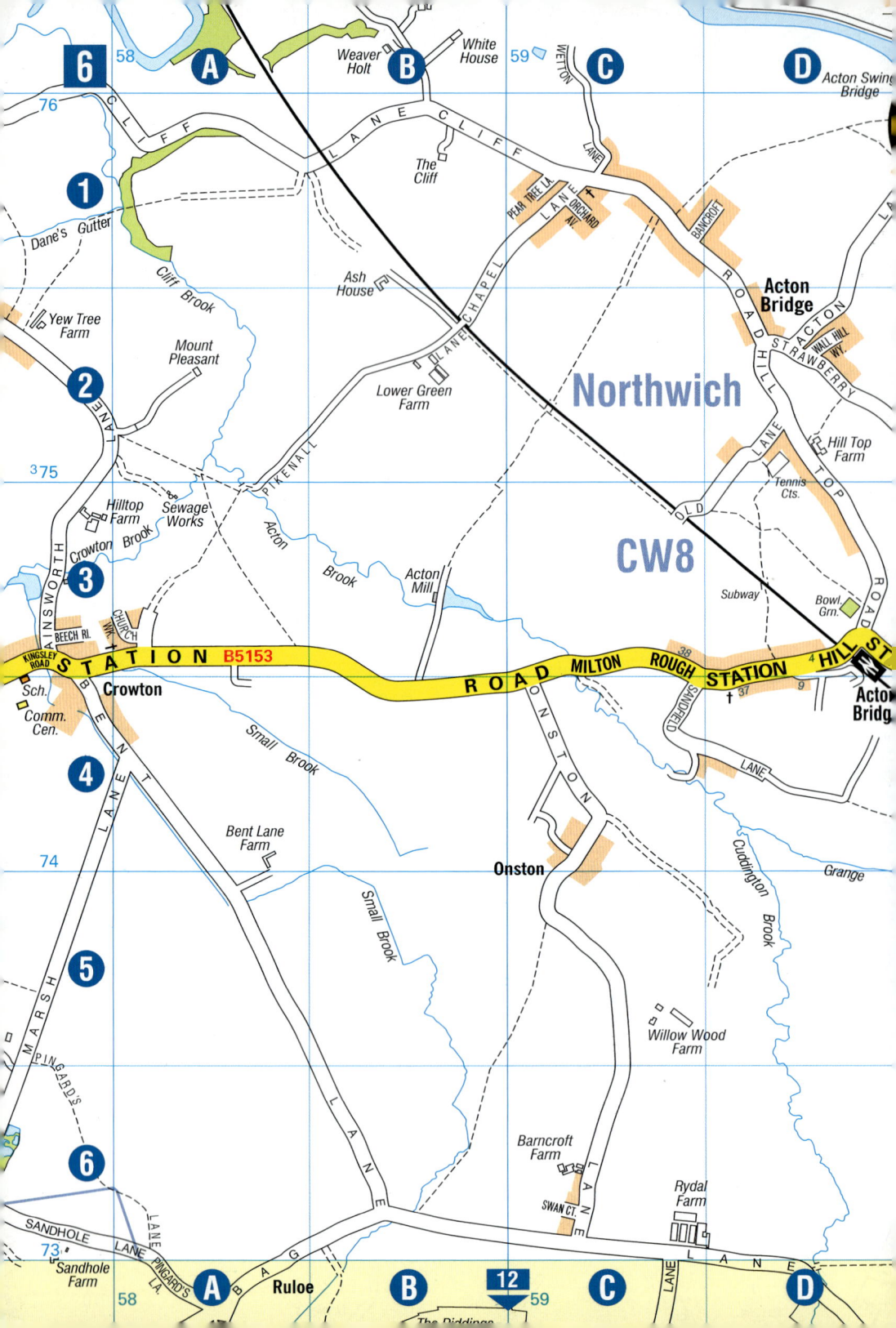

A-Z CREWE

CONTENTS

Map Pages   2-49

Key to Map Pages   Back Cover

Index to Streets, Towns, Villages, Hospitals and Selected Places of Interest   50-68

REFERENCE

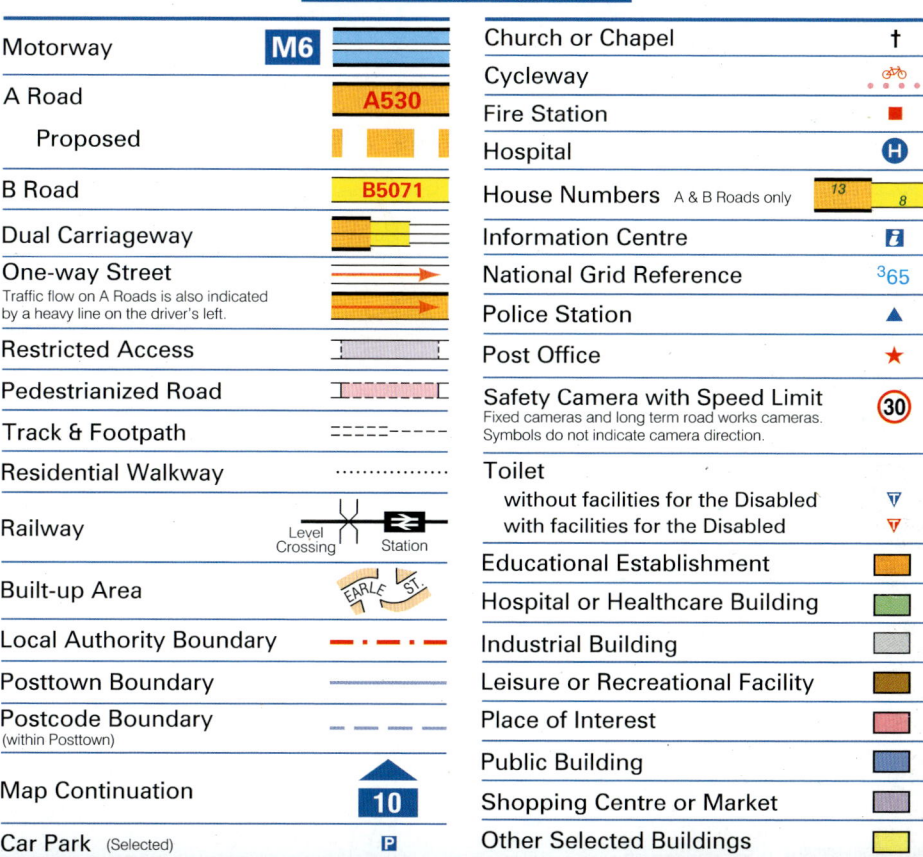

Motorway	**M6**
A Road	**A530**
Proposed	
B Road	**B5071**
Dual Carriageway	
One-way Street	
Traffic flow on A Roads is also indicated by a heavy line on the driver's left.	
Restricted Access	
Pedestrianized Road	
Track & Footpath	
Residential Walkway	
Railway	Level Crossing Station
Built-up Area	EARLE ST.
Local Authority Boundary	
Posttown Boundary	
Postcode Boundary (within Posttown)	
Map Continuation	**10**
Car Park (Selected)	P

Church or Chapel	†
Cycleway	
Fire Station	■
Hospital	**H**
House Numbers A & B Roads only	13 8
Information Centre	**i**
National Grid Reference	³65
Police Station	▲
Post Office	★
Safety Camera with Speed Limit	**30**
Fixed cameras and long term road works cameras. Symbols do not indicate camera direction.	
Toilet	
without facilities for the Disabled	▽
with facilities for the Disabled	▽
Educational Establishment	
Hospital or Healthcare Building	
Industrial Building	
Leisure or Recreational Facility	
Place of Interest	
Public Building	
Shopping Centre or Market	
Other Selected Buildings	

SCALE

1:15,840   4 inches to 1 mile   6.31 cm to 1 km   10.16 cm to 1 mile

0   ¼   ½   ¾   1 Mile

0   250   500   750   1 Kilometre

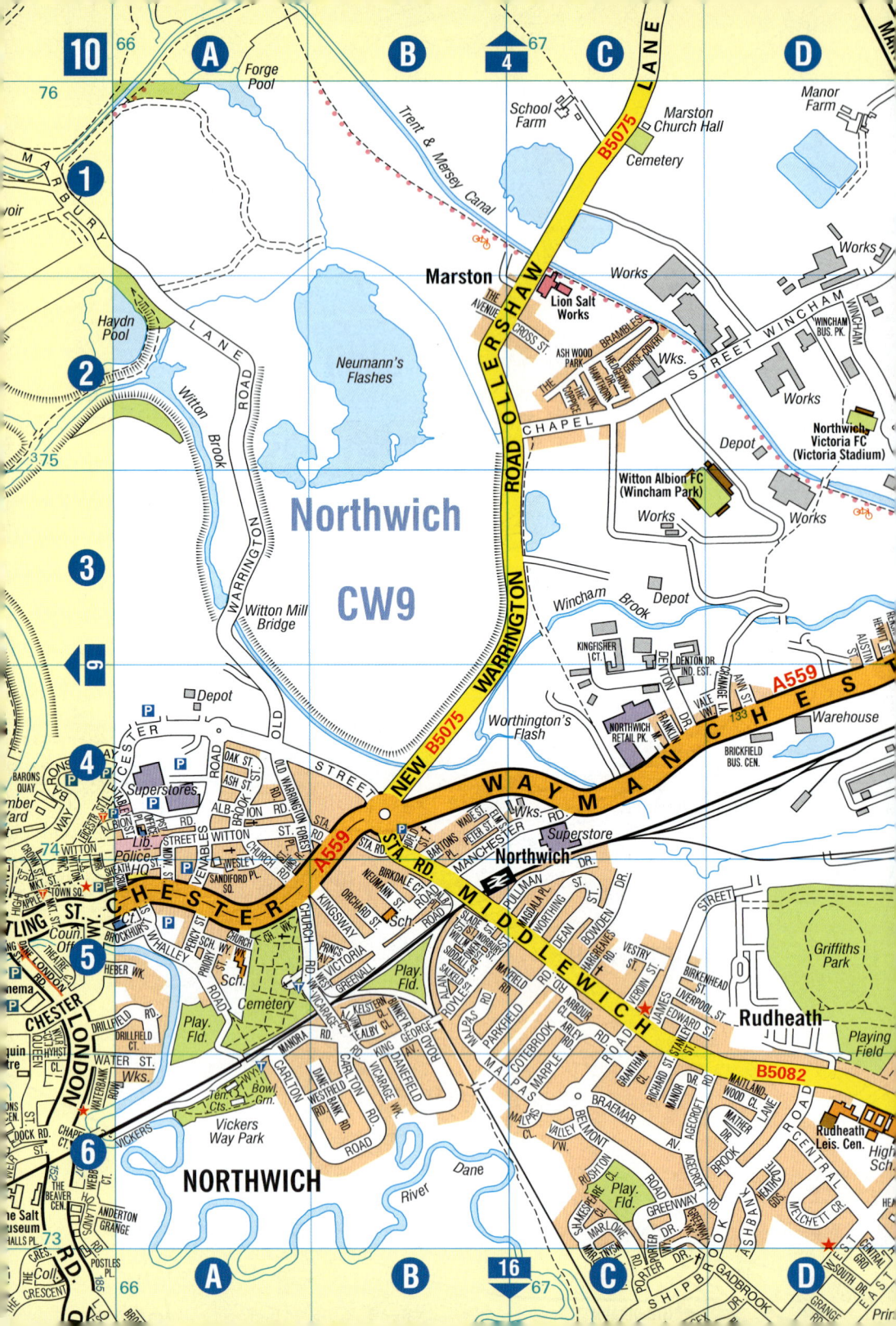

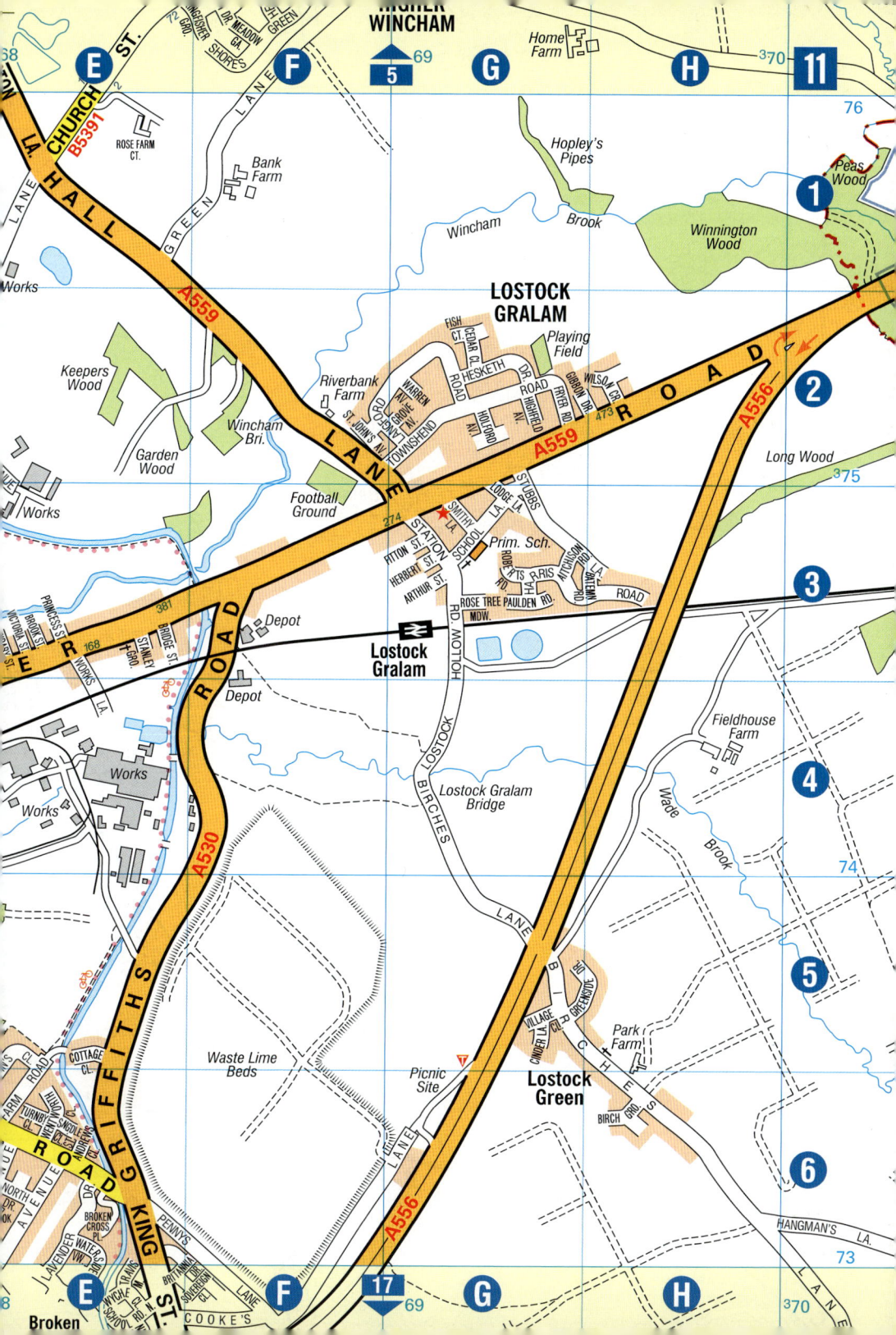

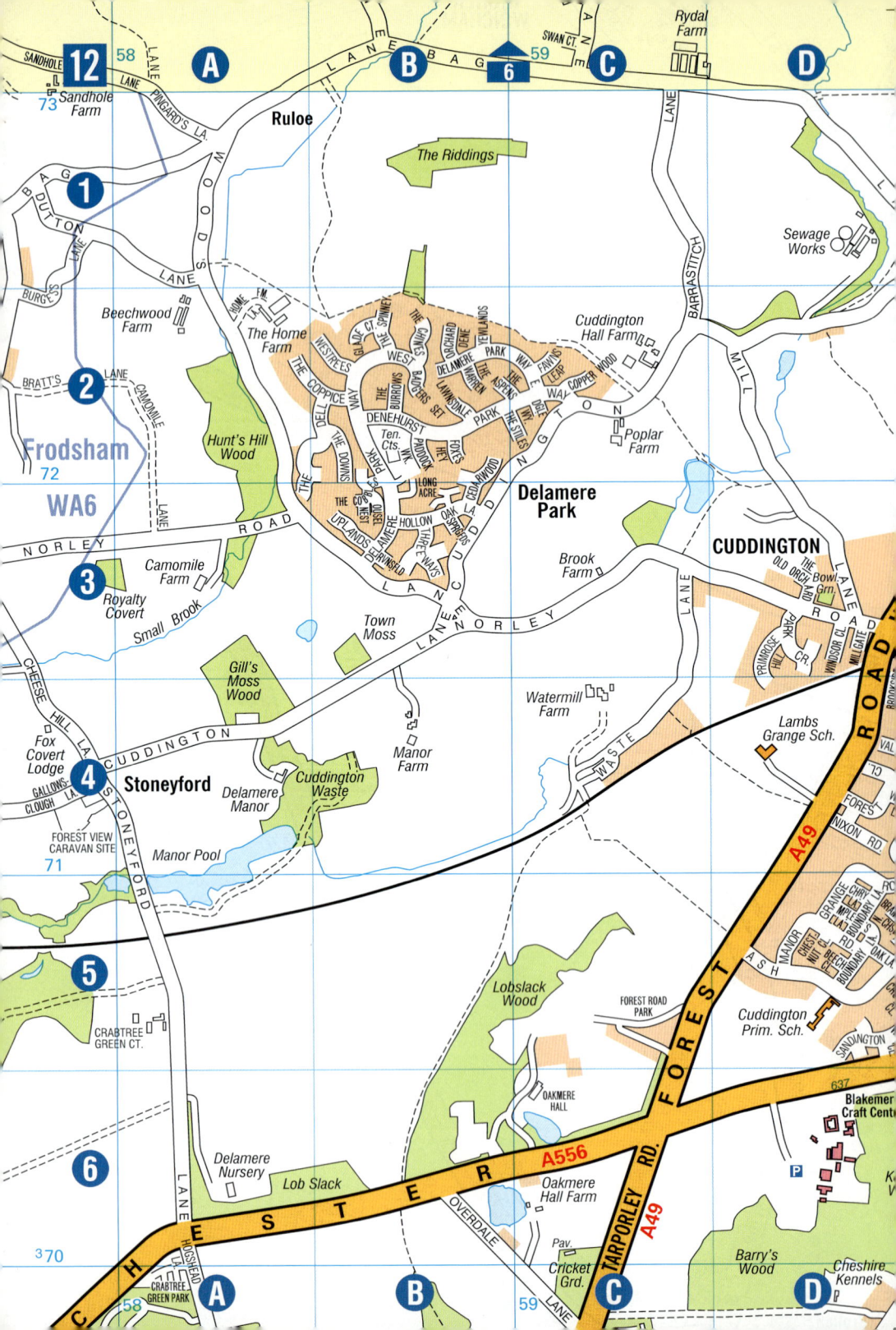

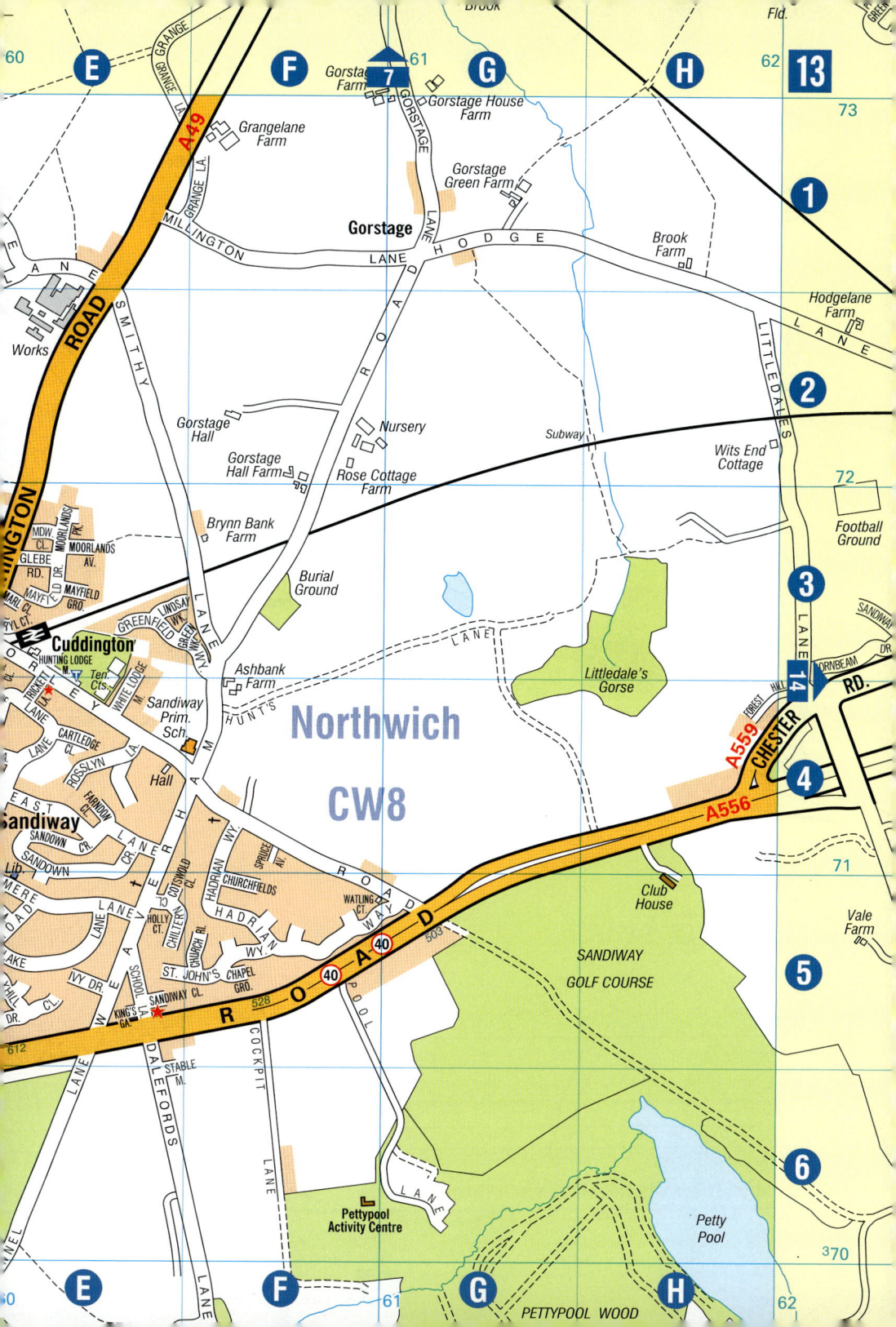

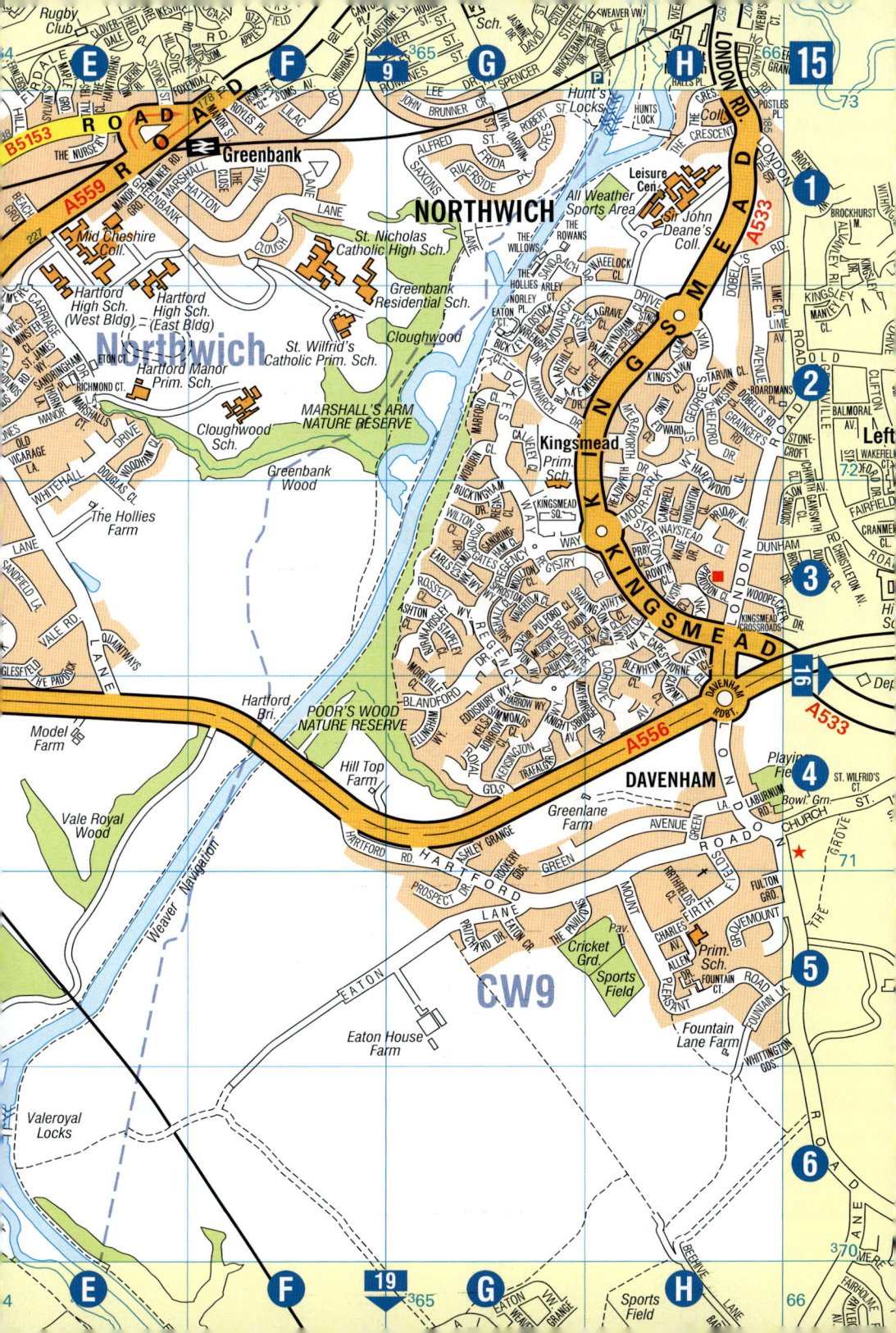

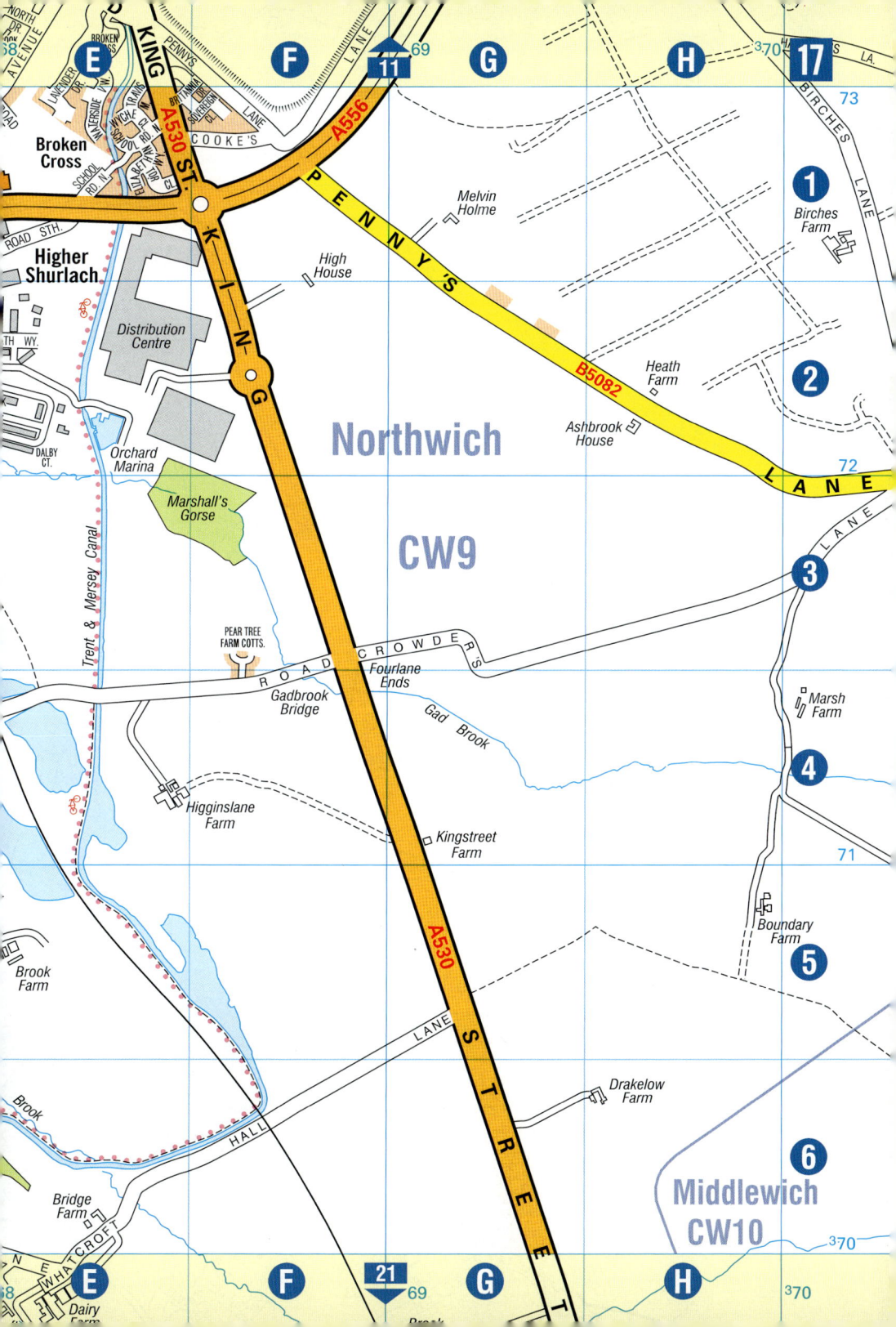

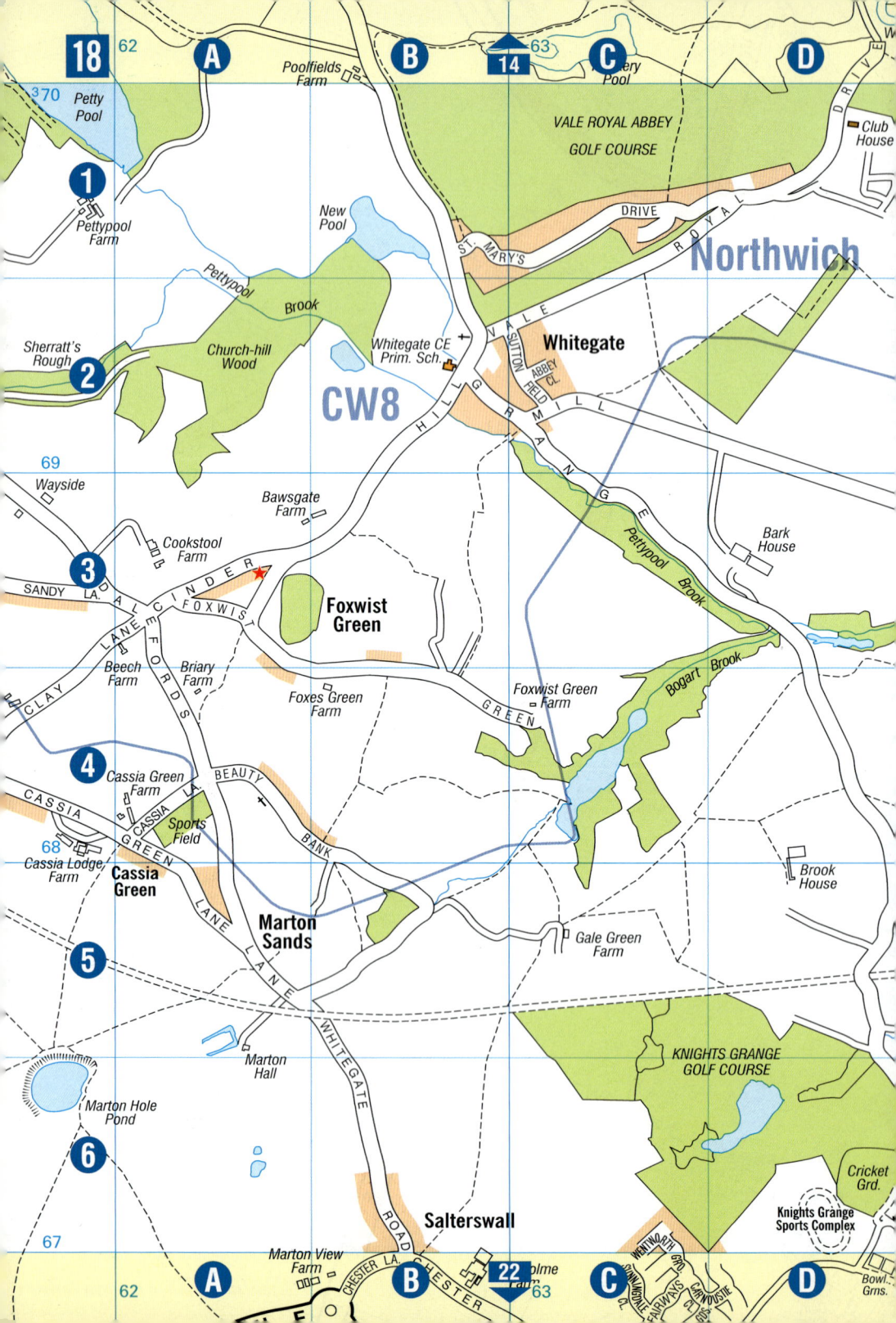

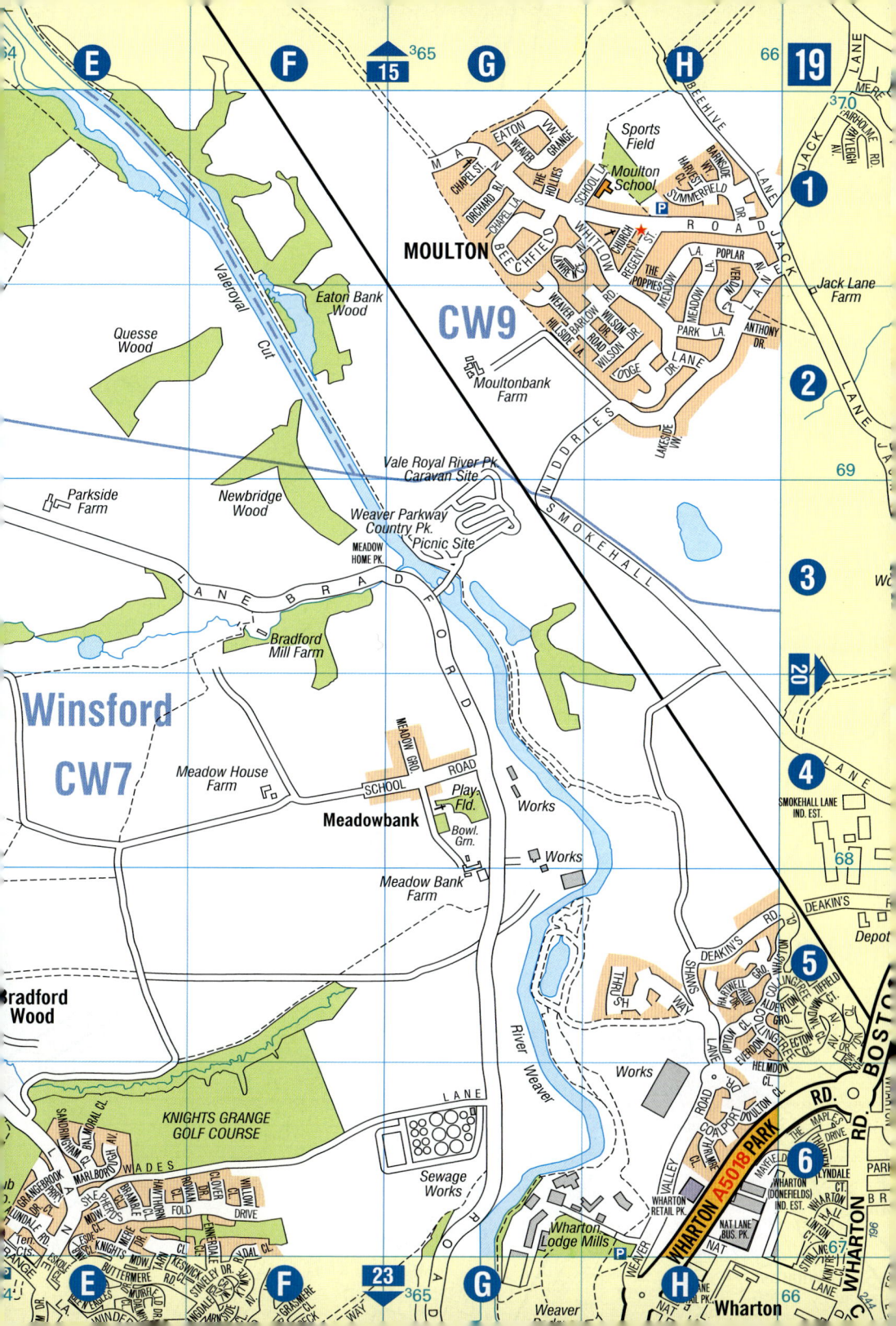

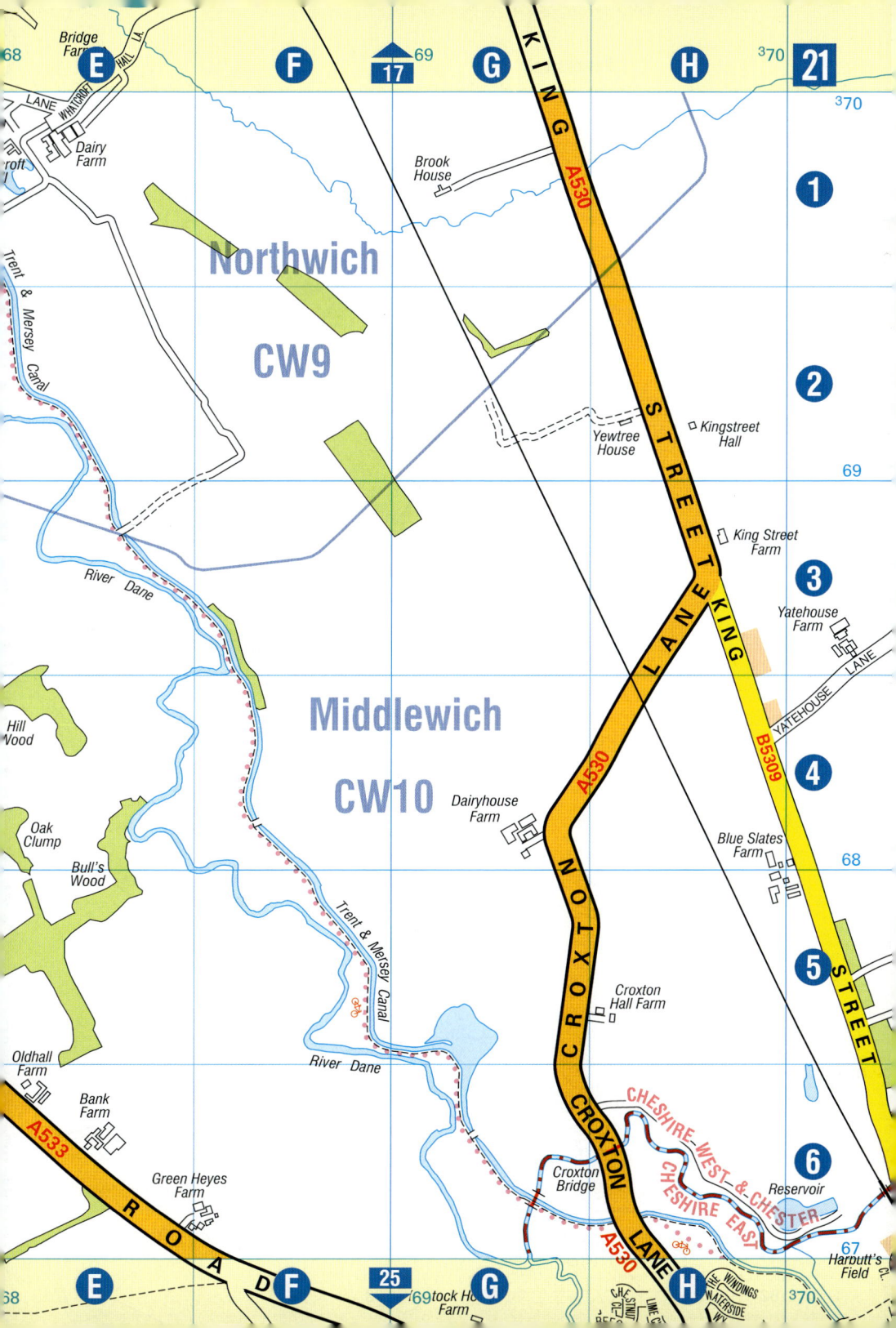

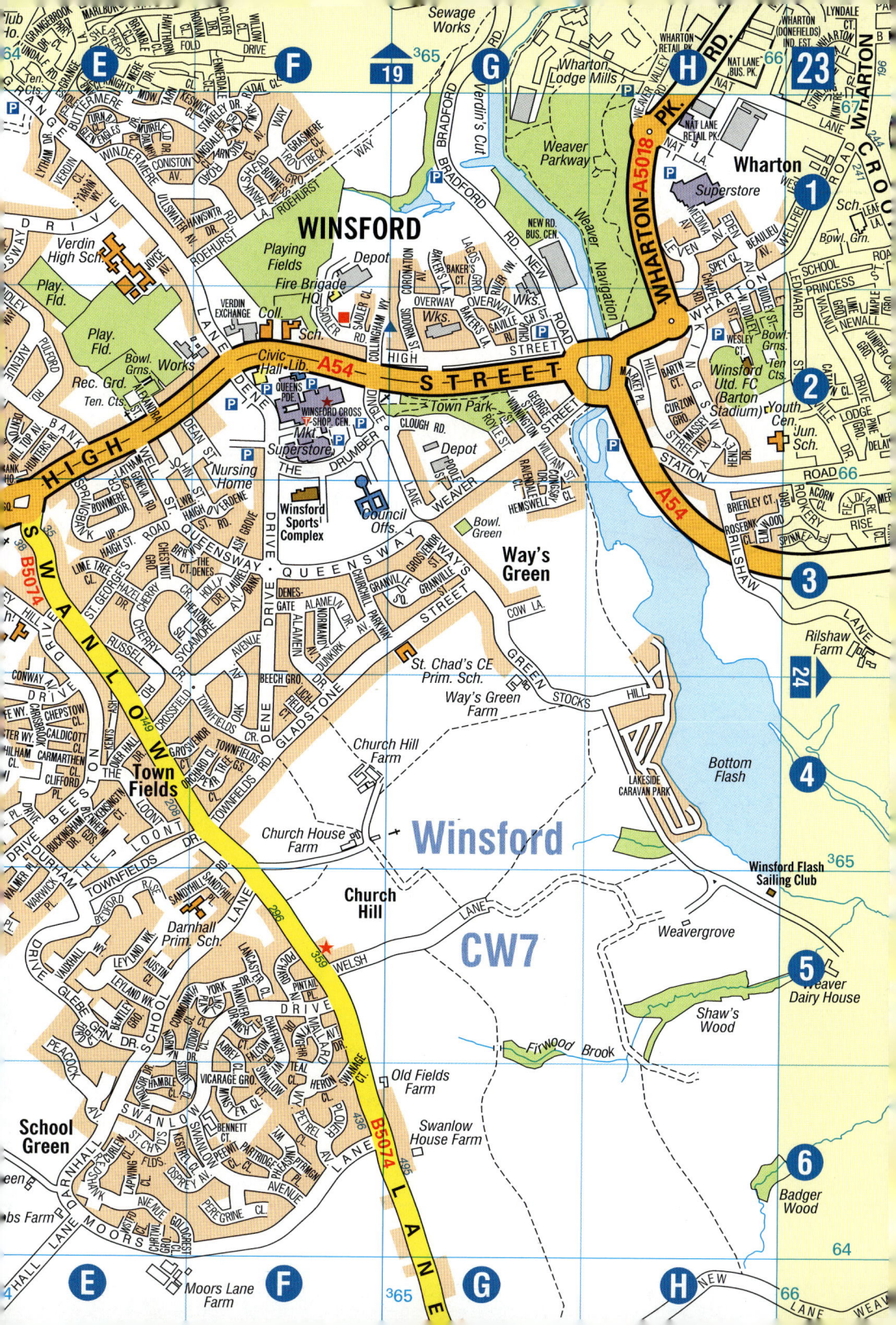

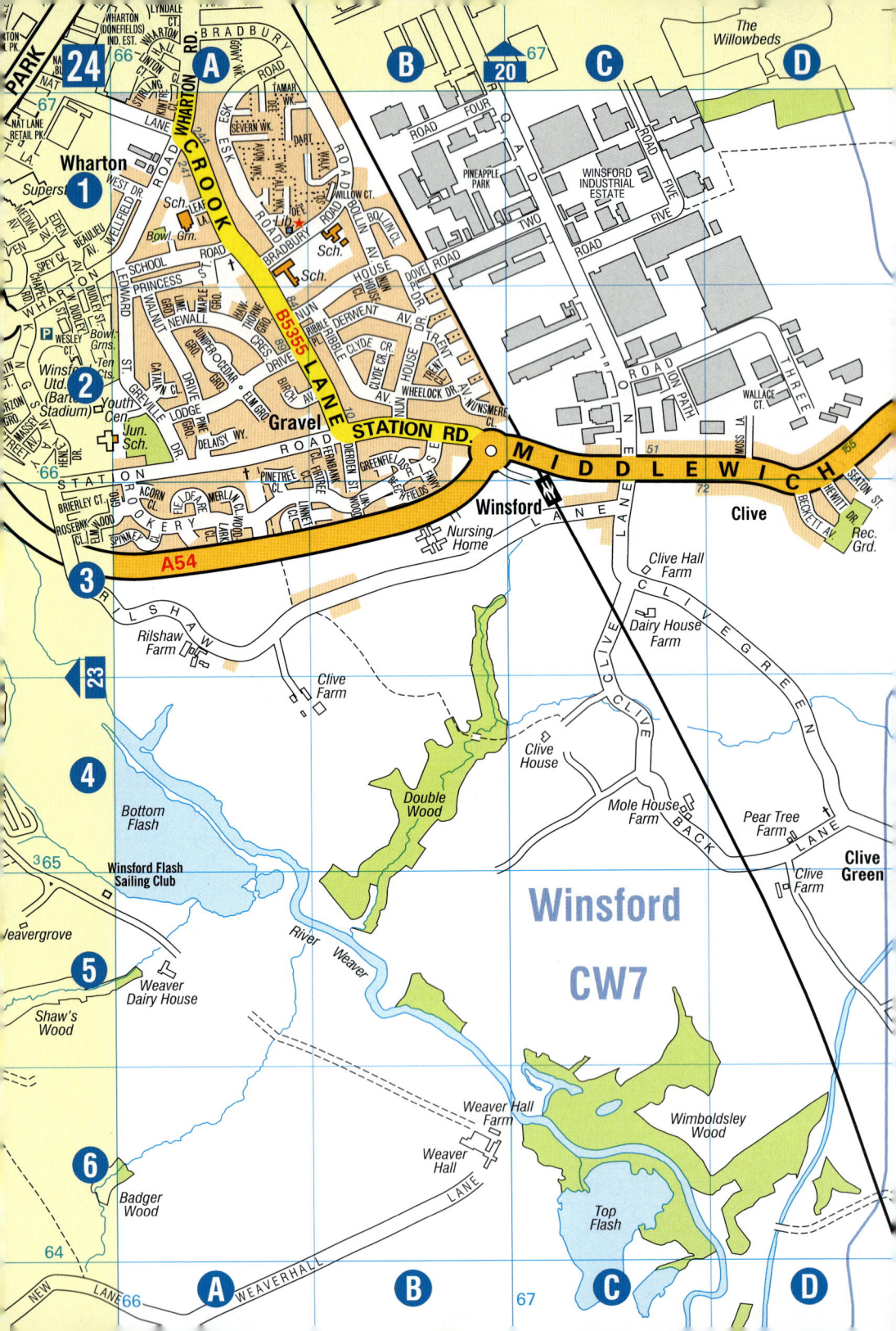

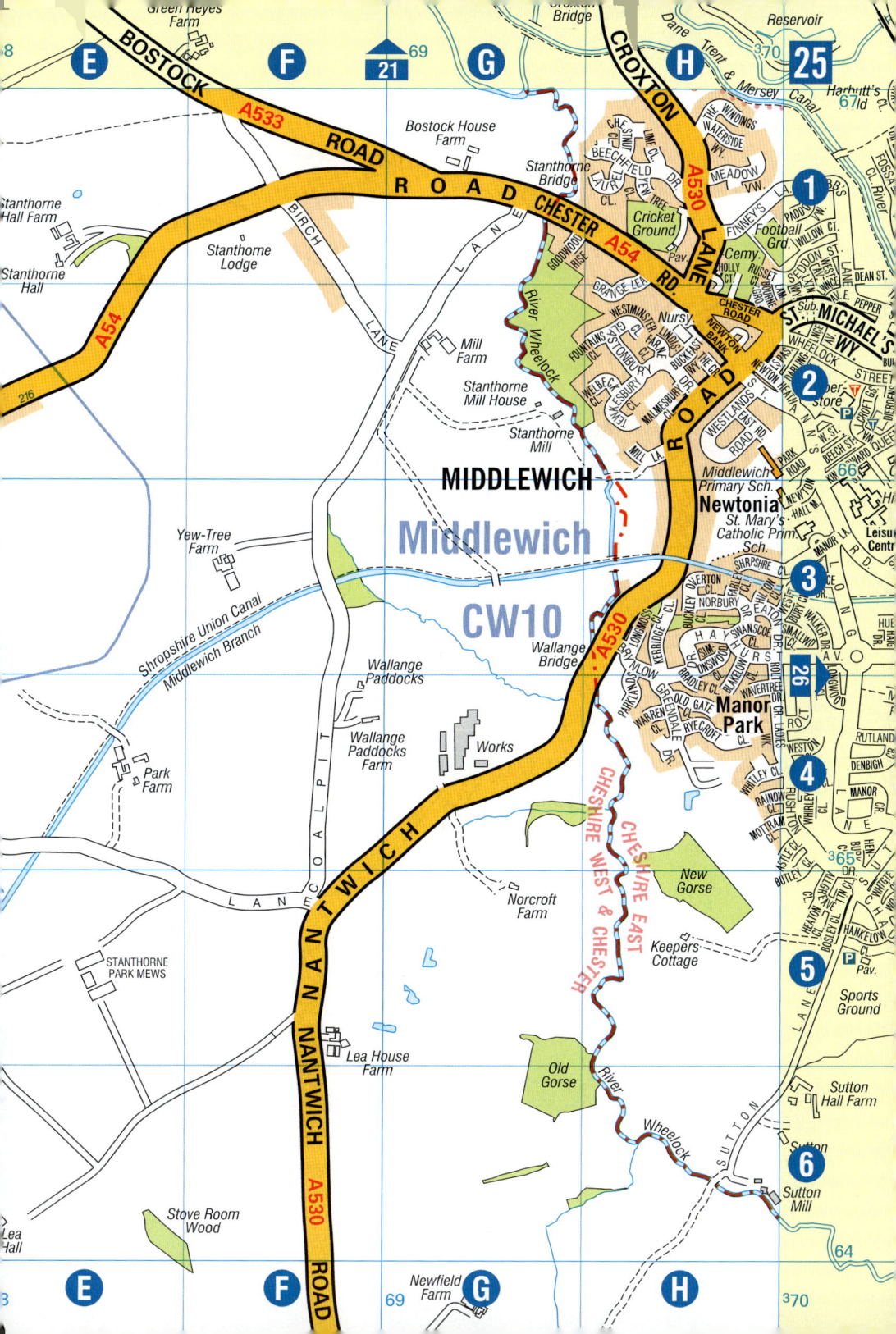

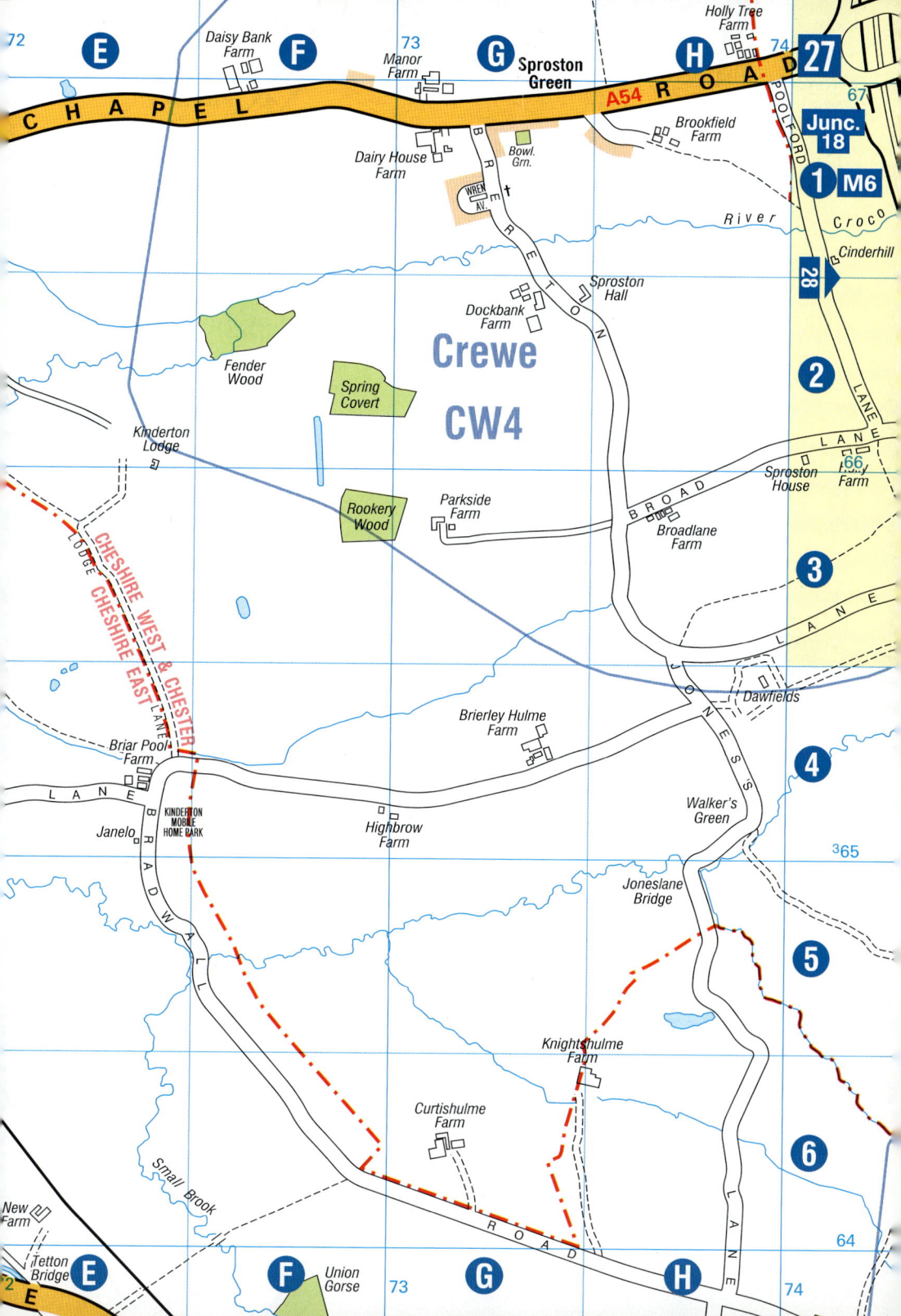

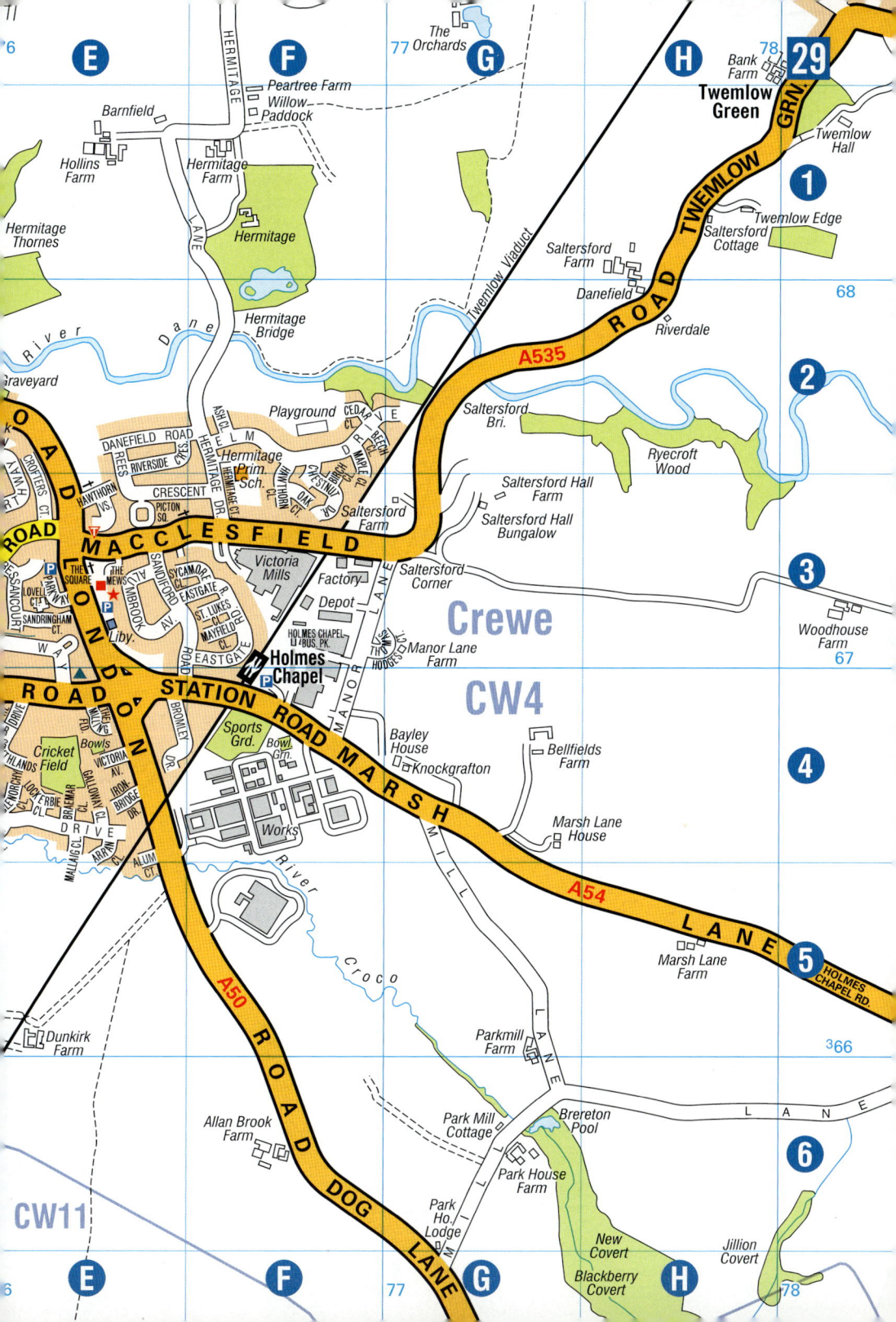

E **F** **G** **H** 78 **29**

77 The Orchards
Bank Farm
Twemlow Green

Peartree Farm
Willow Paddock
Barnfield
Twemlow Hall

Hermitage Farm
Hollins Farm
1

Hermitage Thornes
Hermitage
Twemlow Edge
Saltersford Cottage

TWEMLOW ROAD GRN.

68

Saltersford Farm
Danefield
Riverdale

Hermitage Bridge

River Dane
Saltersford Bri.

A535
2

Graveyard
Ryecroft Wood

Playground

Danefield Road
Riverside
Hermitage Prim. Sch.
Saltersford Hall Farm
3

CRESCENT
Picton Sq.
Saltersford Farm
Saltersford Hall Bungalow

MACCLESFIELD
Victoria Mills
Saltersford Corner
Woodhouse Farm

The Square
The Mews
Eastgate
Factory
Depot
67

Liby.
Holmes Chapel Bus. Pk.
Manor Lane Farm
Crewe

Holmes Chapel
CW4

STATION ROAD
Bayley House
Bellfields Farm
4

Cricket Field
Sports Grd.
Bowls
Bowl Grn.
Knockgrafton

Works
Marsh Lane House

River Croco
MARSH LANE
Marsh Lane Farm
A54
5

HOLMES CHAPEL RD.

A50 ROAD
Parkmill Farm
366

Dunkirk Farm
MILL LANE

Allan Brook Farm
Park Mill Cottage
Brereton Pool
LANE
6

CW11
Park Ho. Lodge
Park House Farm

DOG LANE
New Covert
Jillion Covert

E **F** **G** Blackberry Covert **H** 78

77

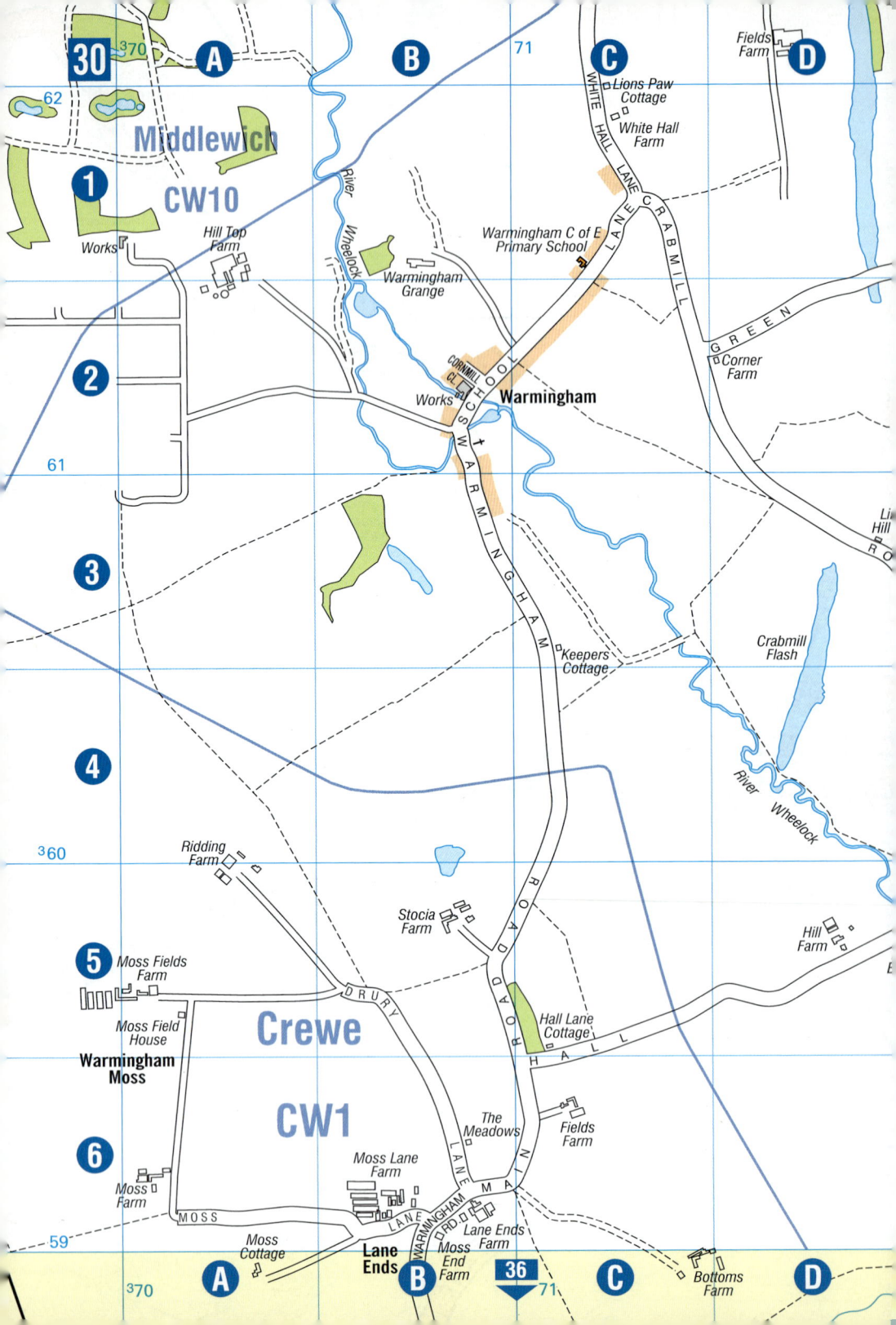

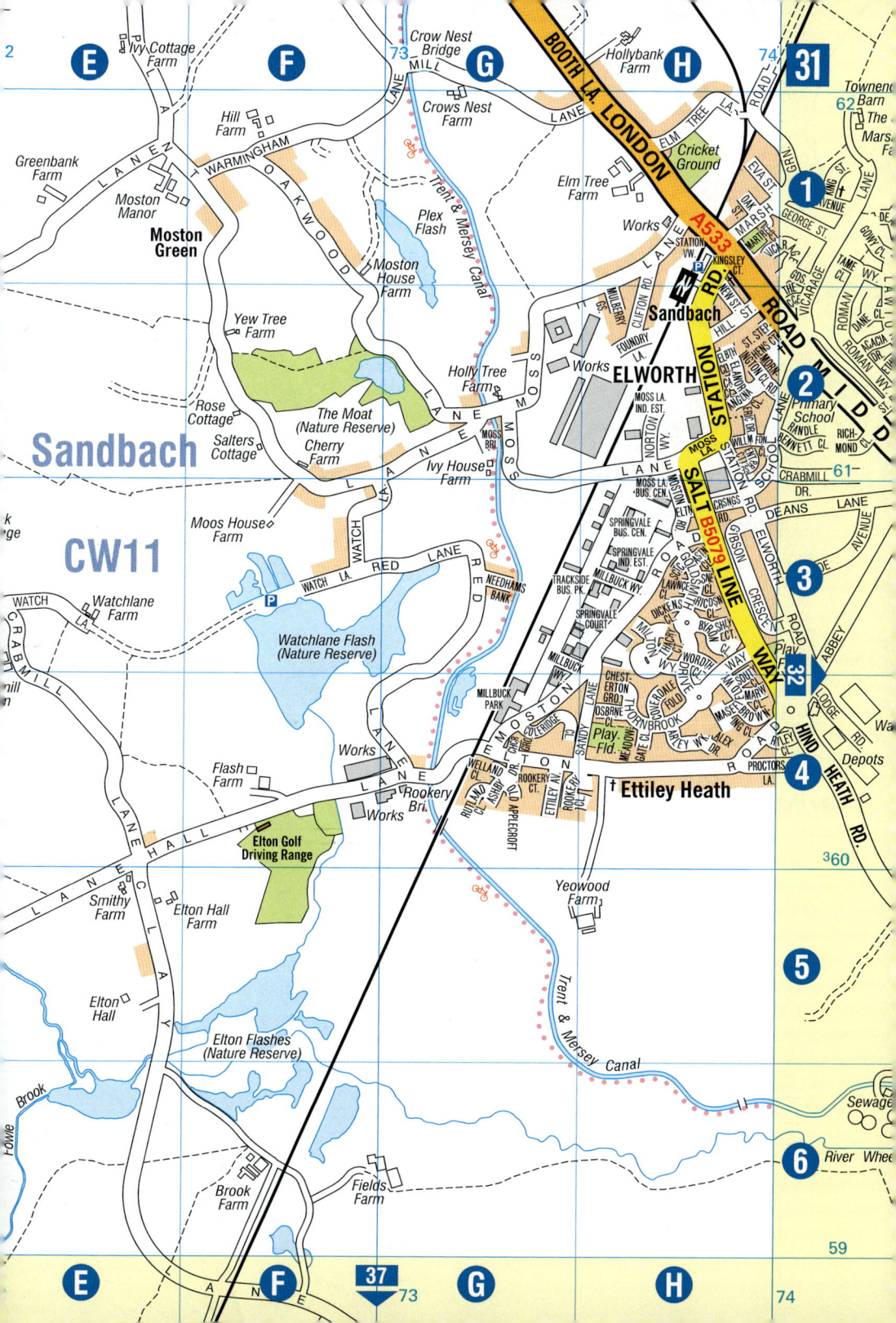

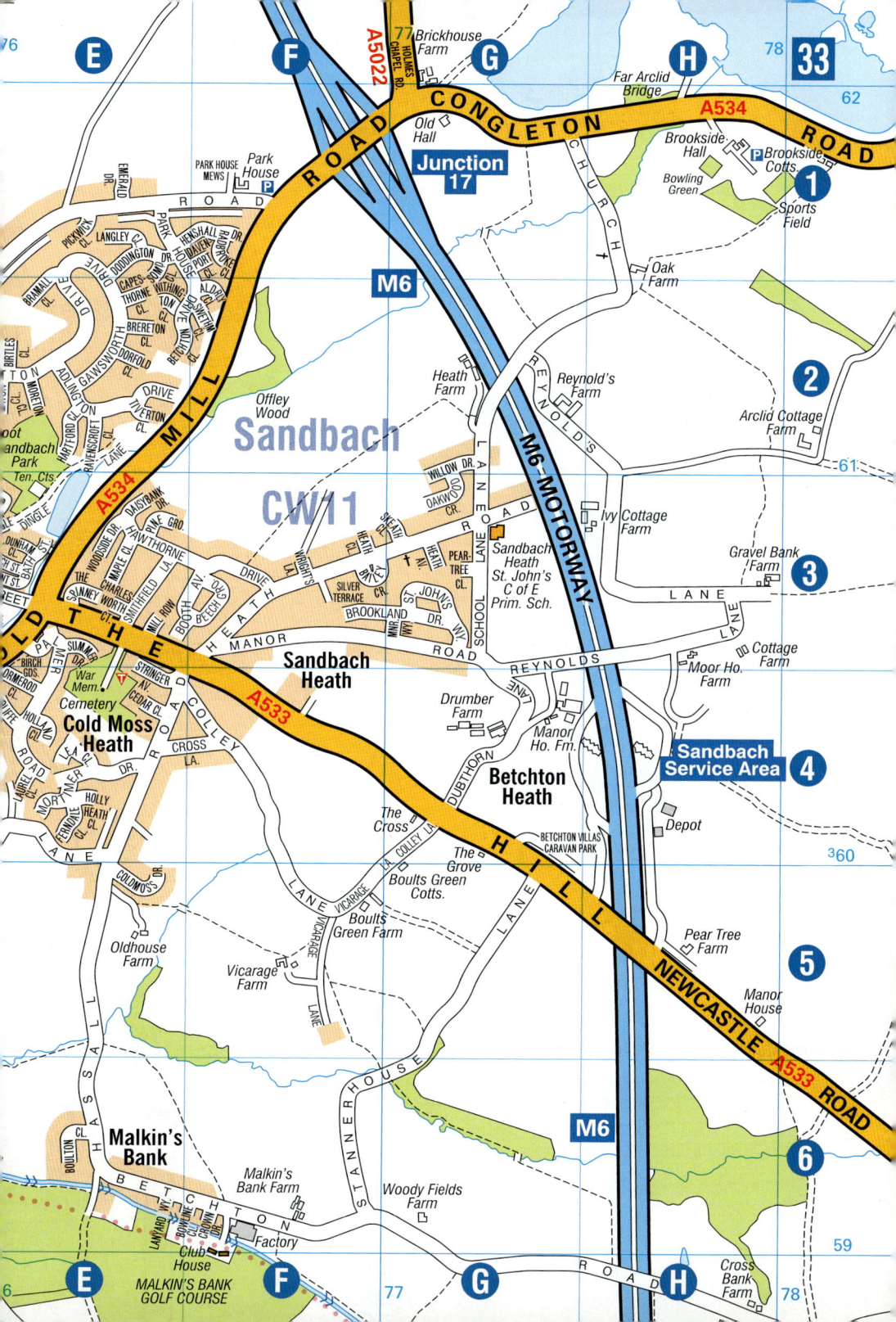

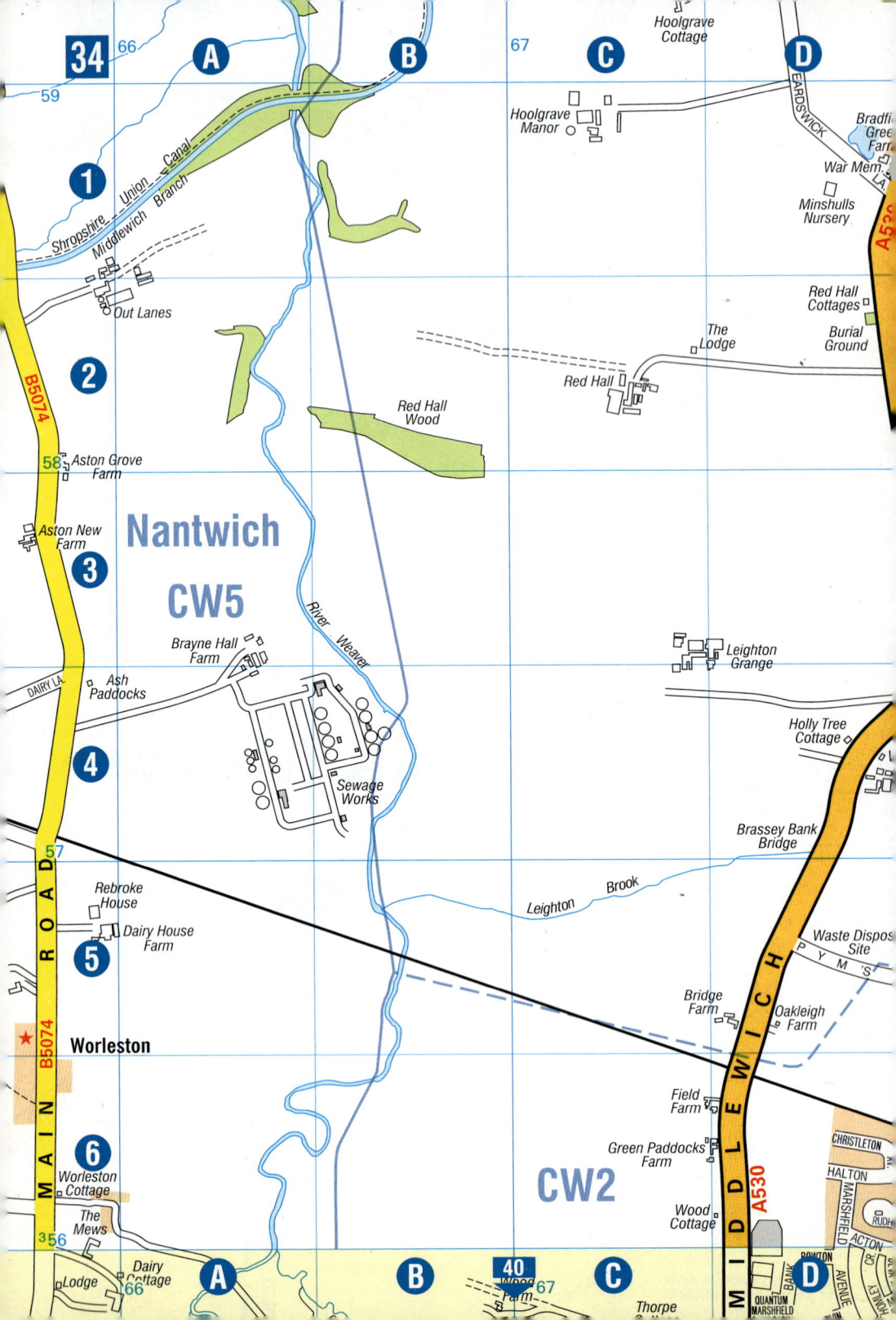

66 59

A **B** 67 **C** **D**

1

Shropshire Union Canal

Middlewich Branch

Hoolgrave Cottage

Hoolgrave Manor

EARDSWICK

Bradfi Gree Farm

War Mem

A530

Out Lanes

2

58

Aston Grove Farm

Minshulls Nursery

Red Hall Cottages

Burial Ground

The Lodge

Red Hall Wood

Red Hall

Aston New Farm

3

Nantwich

CW5

River Weaver

Brayne Hall Farm

Leighton Grange

DAIRY LA

Ash Paddocks

B5074

Holly Tree Cottage

4

Sewage Works

Brassey Bank Bridge

57

Leighton Brook

Waste Dispos Site

Rebroke House

P Y M 'S

Dairy House Farm

5

Bridge Farm

Oakleigh Farm

B5074

Worleston

MAIN ROAD

Field Farm

A530

Green Paddocks Farm

CW2

CHRISTLETON

HALTON

MARSHFIELD

ACTON

RUDH

6

Worleston Cottage

Wood Cottage

MIDDLEWICH

BANK

The Mews

356

Lodge

Dairy Cottage

A

66

B

40
Wood Farm
67

C

Thorpe

BOWTON

QUANTUM MARSHFIELD

D

AVENUE

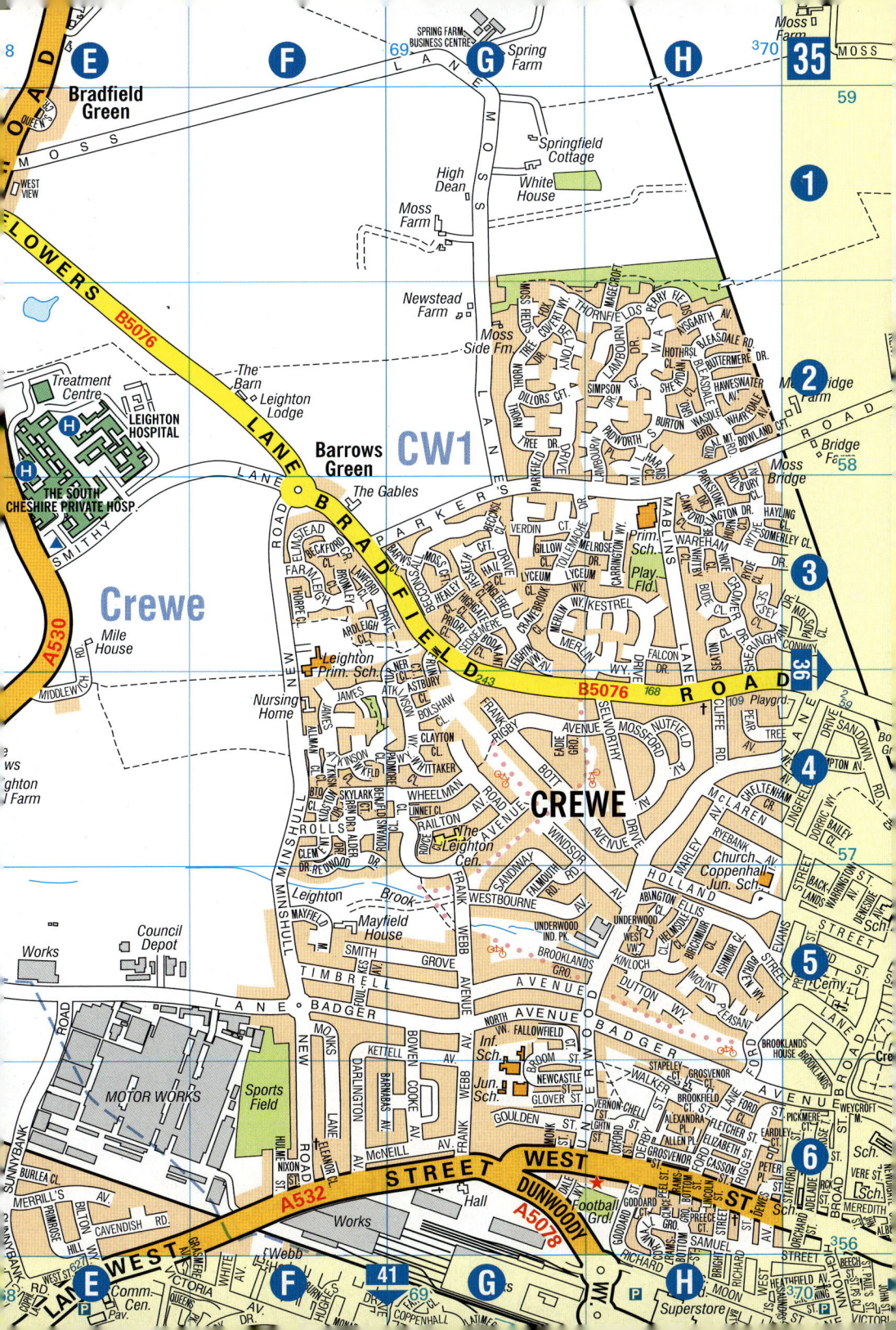

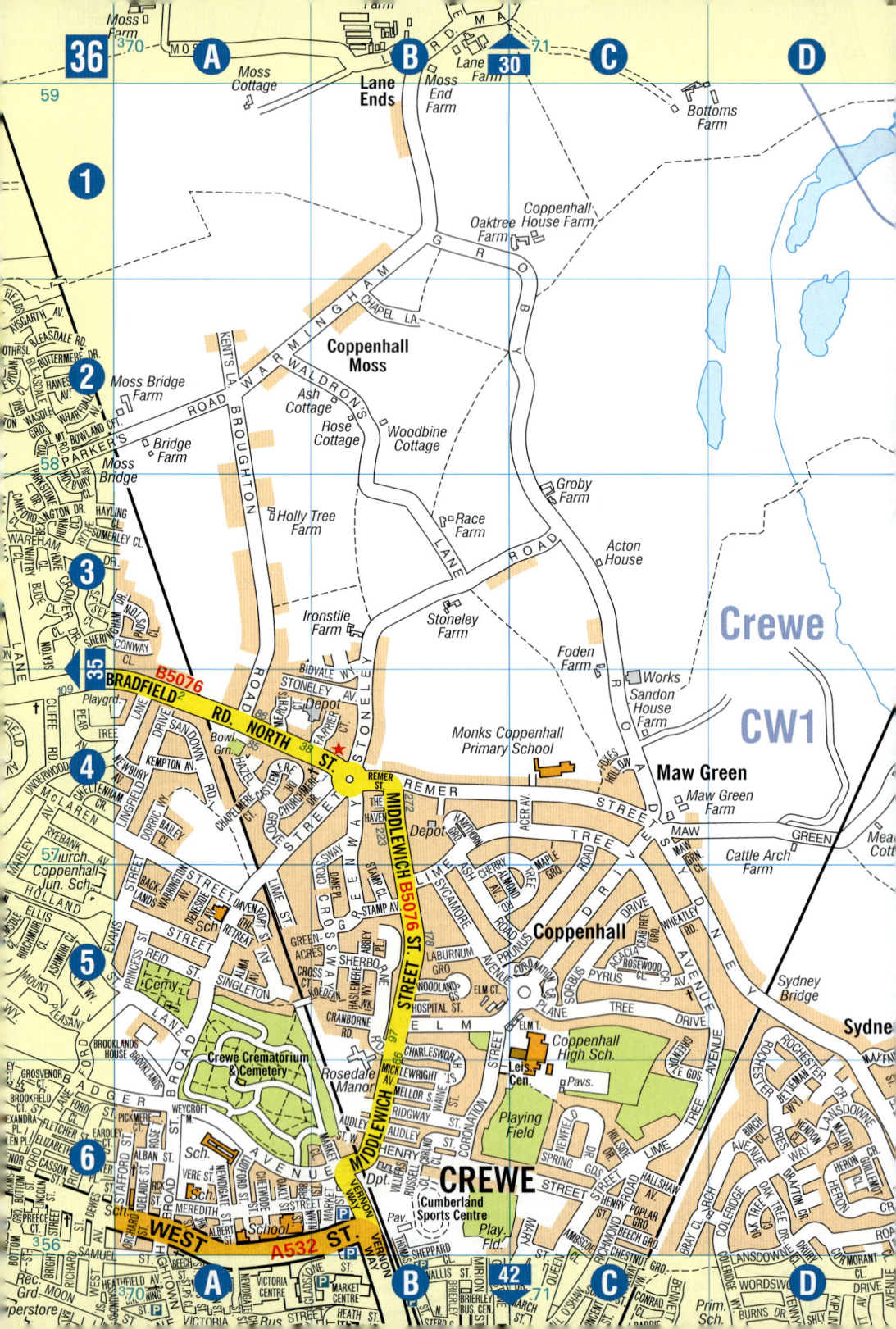

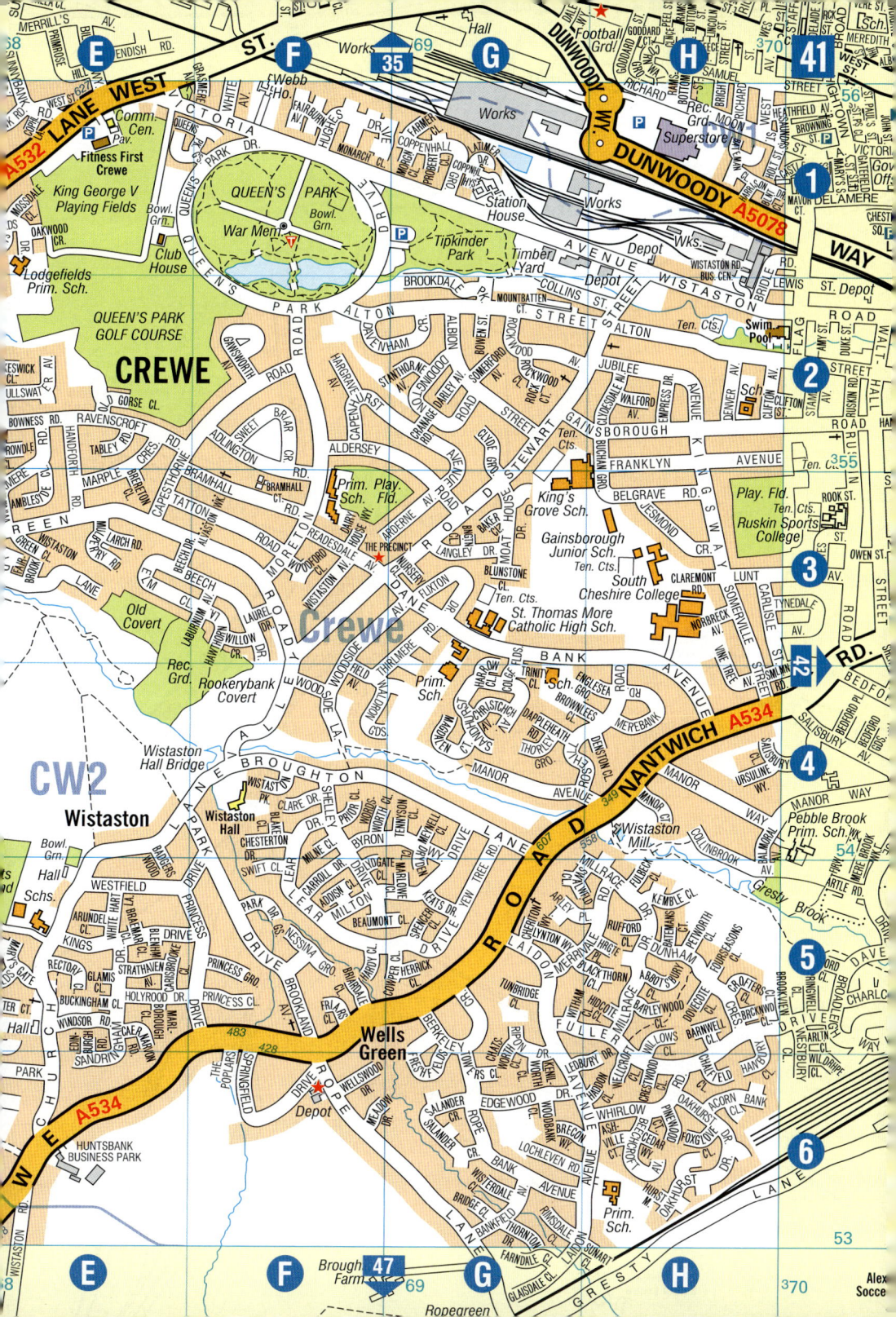

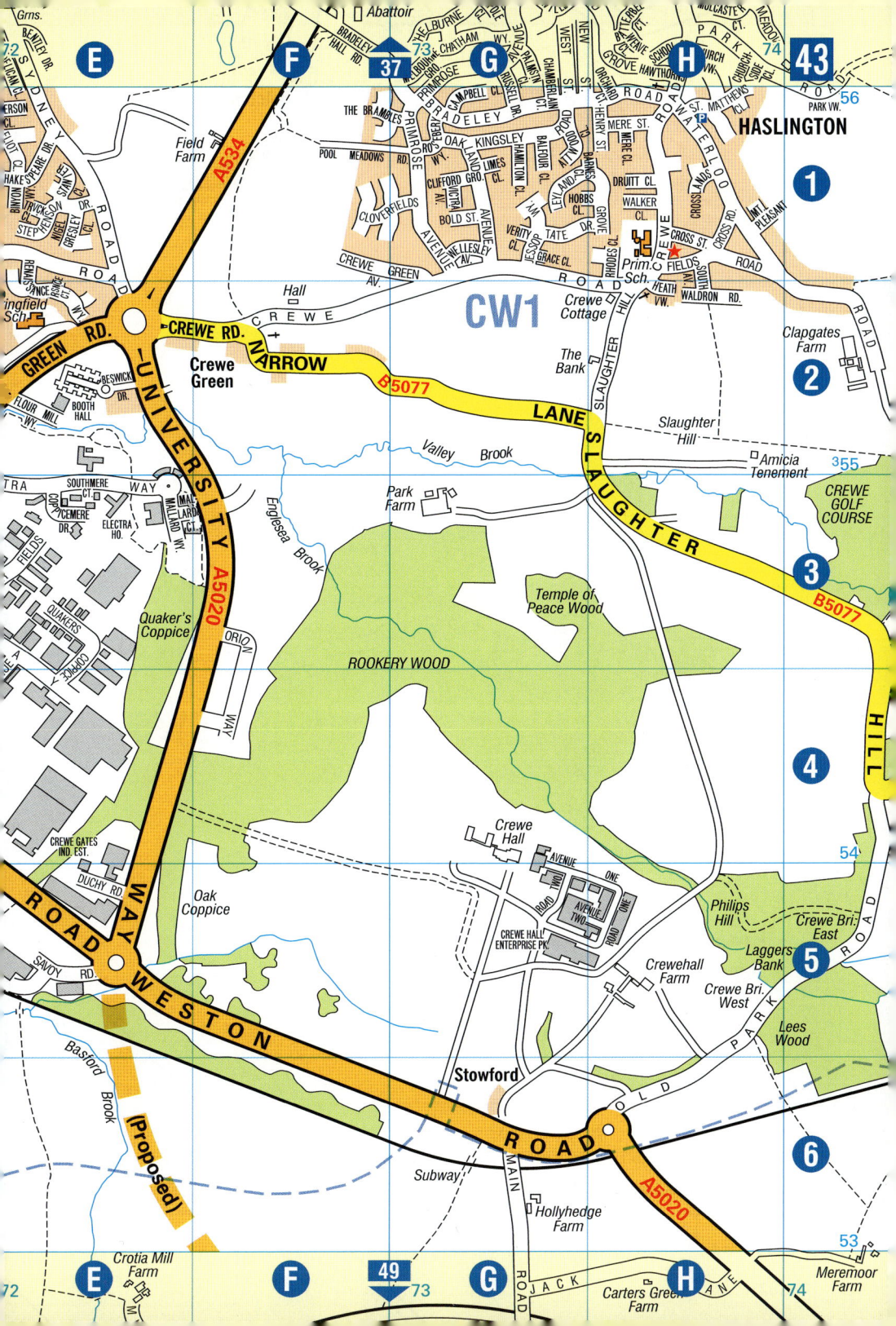

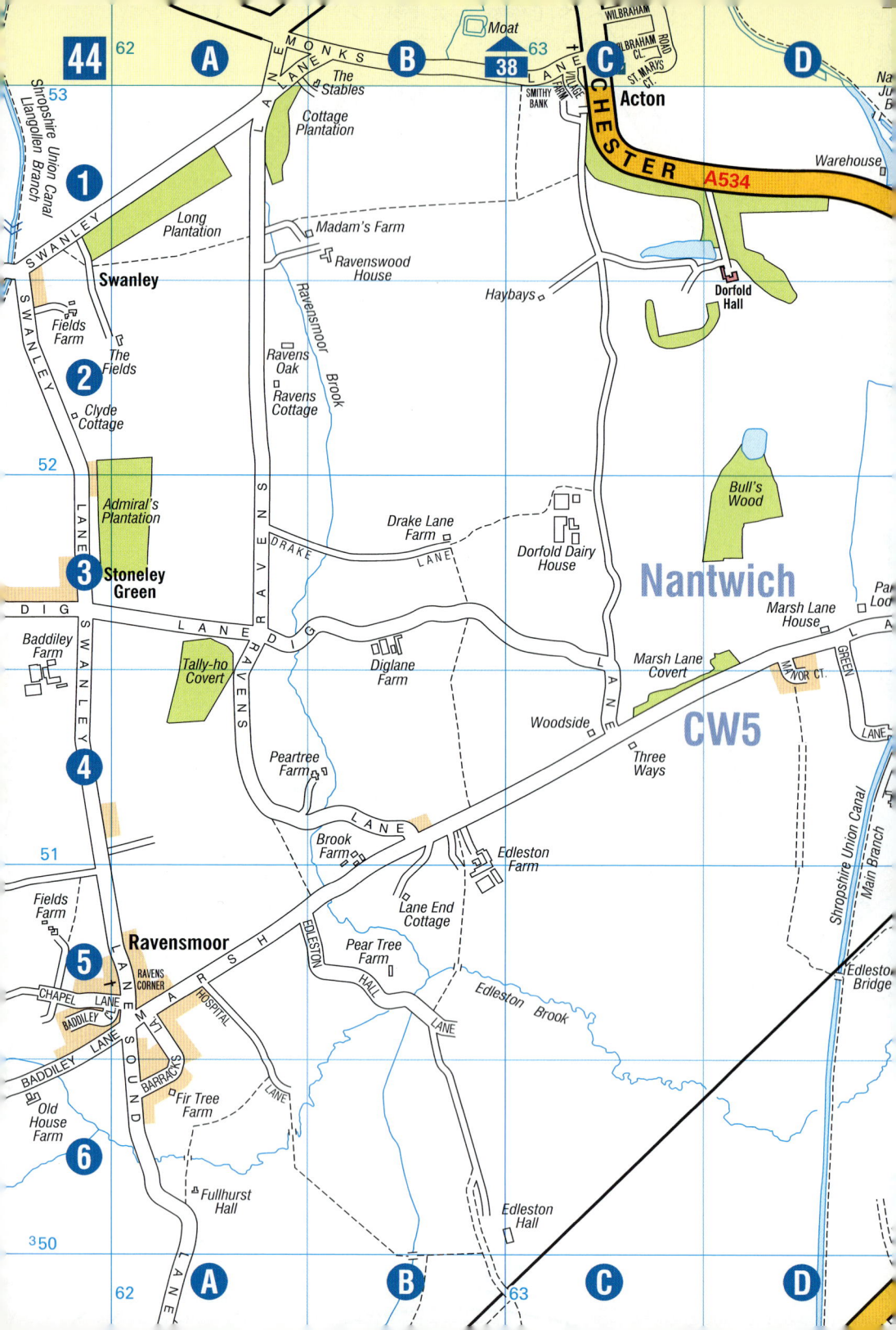

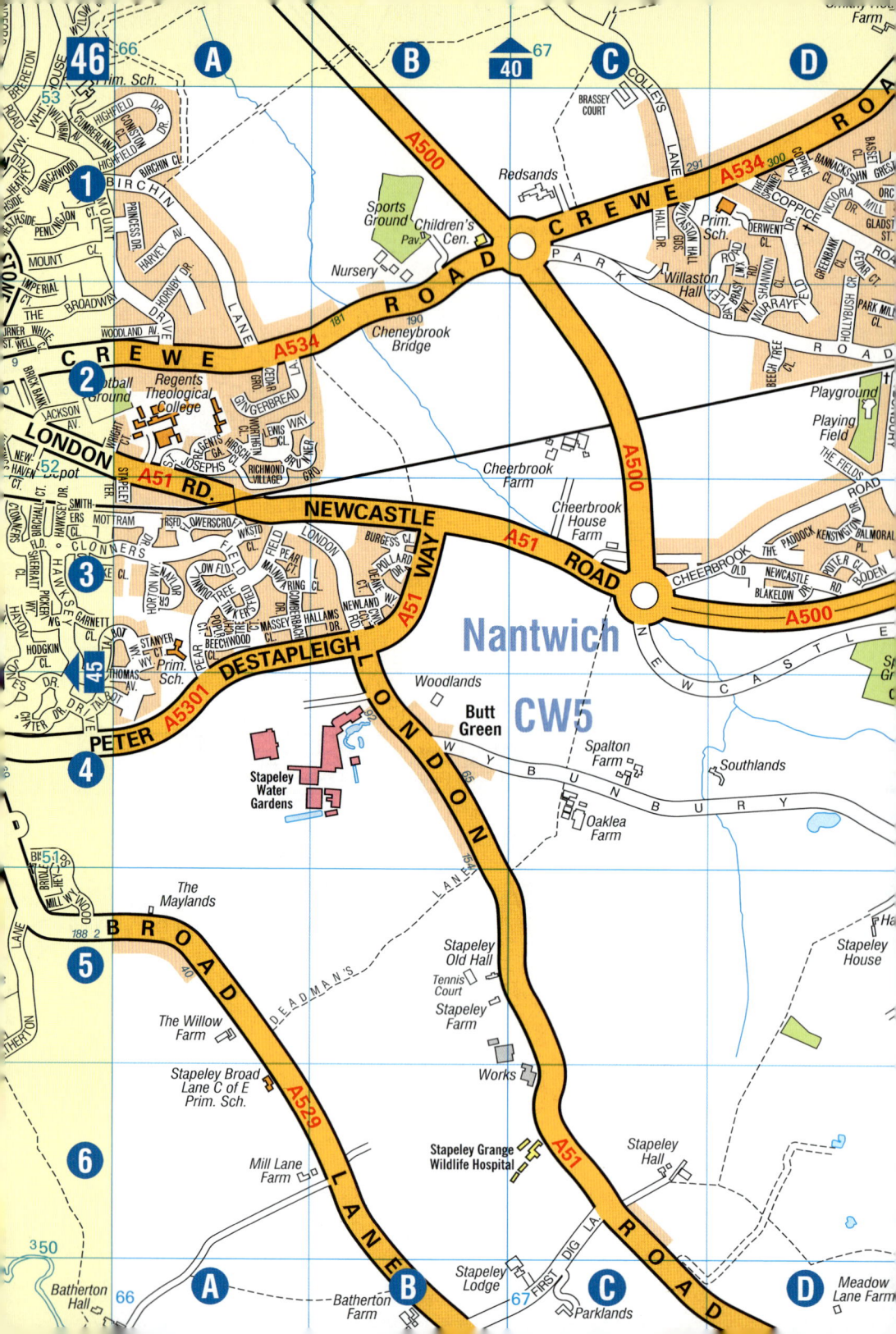

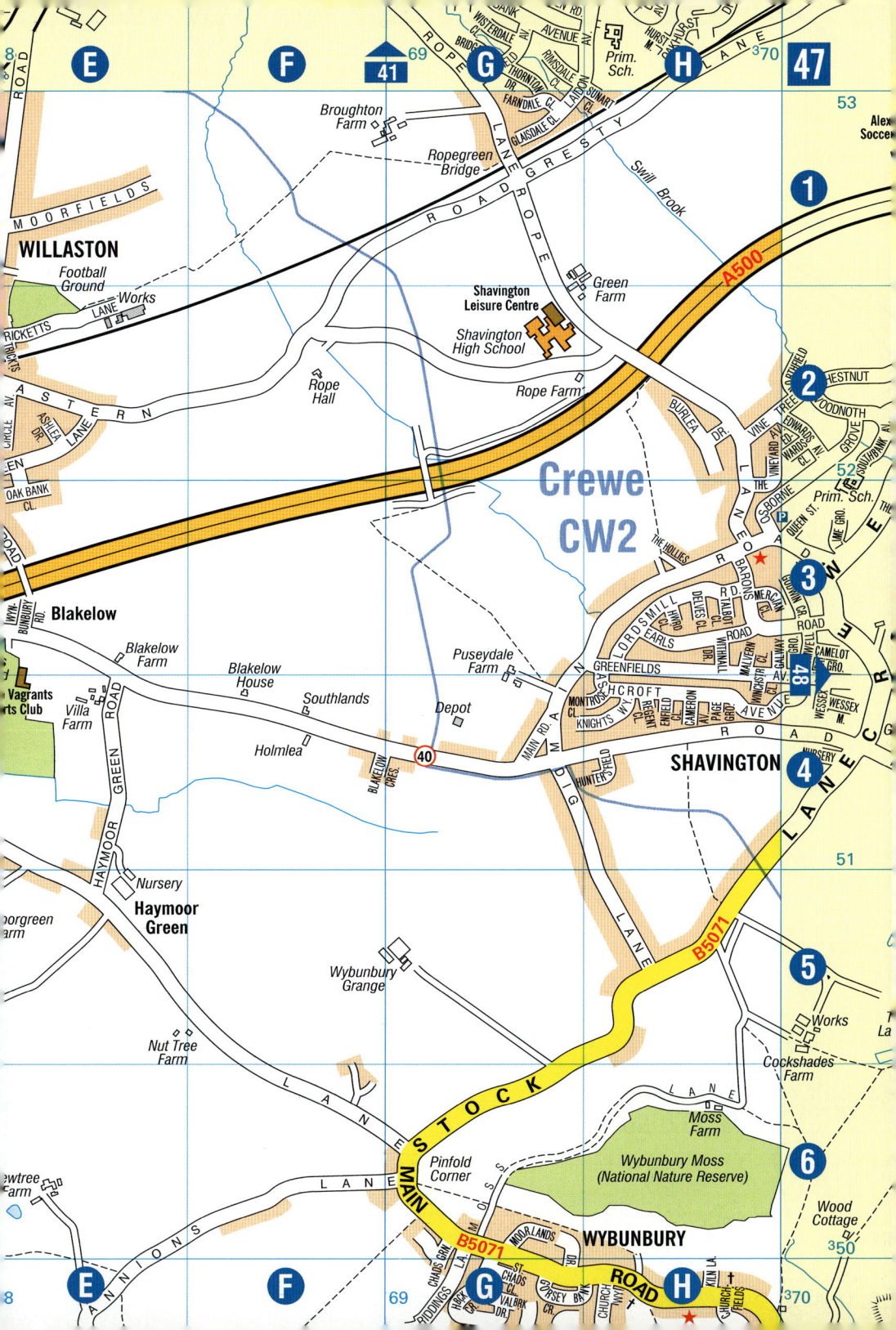

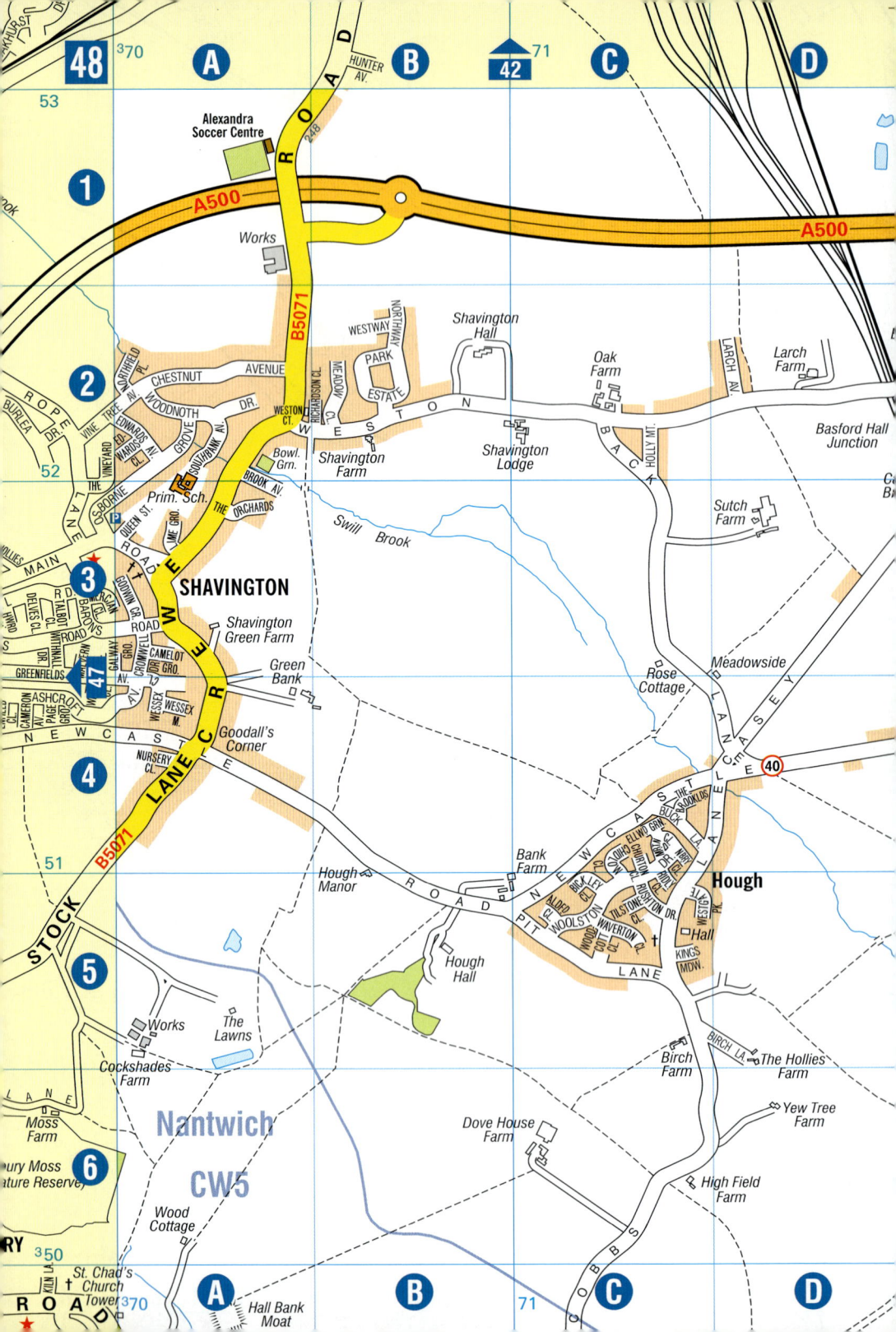

INDEX

Including Streets, Places & Areas, Hospitals, Industrial Estates,
Selected Flats & Walkways, Service Areas, Stations and Selected Places of Interest.

HOW TO USE THIS INDEX

1. Each street name is followed by its Postcode District, then by its Locality abbreviation(s) and then by its map reference;
e.g. **Abbey Rd.** CW11: Sandb . . . .3A **42** is in the CW11 Postcode District and the Sandbach Locality and is to be found in square 3A on page **42**. The page number is shown in bold type.

2. A strict alphabetical order is followed in which Av., Rd., St., etc. (though abbreviated) are read in full and as part of the street name; e.g. **Brook La.** appears after **Brooklands Ho.** but before **Brooklyn St.**

3. Streets and a selection of flats and walkways too small to be shown on the maps, appear in the index with the thoroughfare to which it is connected shown in brackets; e.g. **Abbots Mere Cl.** CW8: Sandi . . . .5D **12** (off Sandington Dr.)

4. Addresses that are in more than one part are referred to as not continuous.

5. Places and areas are shown in the index in BLUE TYPE and the map reference is to the actual map square in which the town centre or area is located and not to the place name shown on the map; e.g. CASSIA GREEN 4A 18

6. An example of a selected place of interest is Nantwich Mus. 2G 45

7. An example of a station is Acton Bridge Station (Rail) 3D 6

8. Service Areas are shown in the index in BOLD CAPITAL TYPE; e.g. SANDBACH SERVICE AREA 4H 33

9. An example of a Hospital is LEIGHTON HOSPITAL 2E 35

GENERAL ABBREVIATIONS

All. : Alley	**Flds.** : Fields	**Pde.** : Parade
App. : Approach	**Gdns.** : Gardens	**Pk.** : Park
Arc. : Arcade	**Ga.** : Gate	**Pas.** : Passage
Av. : Avenue	**Grn.** : Green	**Pl.** : Place
Bk. : Back	**Gro.** : Grove	**Ri.** : Rise
Bri. : Bridge	**Hgts.** : Heights	**Rd.** : Road
Bldgs. : Buildings	**Ho.** : House	**Rdbt.** : Roundabout
Bus. : Business	**Ind.** : Industrial	**Shop.** : Shopping
Cvn. : Caravan	**Info.** : Information	**Sth.** : South
Cen. : Centre	**Junc.** : Junction	**Sq.** : Square
Cl. : Close	**La.** : Lane	**St.** : Street
Cnr. : Corner	**Lit.** : Little	**Ter.** : Terrace
Cotts. : Cottages	**Lwr.** : Lower	**Trad.** : Trading
Ct. : Court	**Mnr.** : Manor	**Up.** : Upper
Cres. : Crescent	**Mkt.** : Market	**Vw.** : View
Cft. : Croft	**Mdw.** : Meadow	**Vs.** : Villas
Dr. : Drive	**Mdws.** : Meadows	**Wlk.** : Walk
E. : East	**M.** : Mews	**W.** : West
Ent. : Enterprise	**Mt.** : Mount	**Yd.** : Yard
Est. : Estate	**Mus.** : Museum	
Fld. : Field	**Nth.** : North	

LOCALITY ABBREVIATIONS

Act : **Acton**	Dave : **Davenham**	Oak : **Oakmere**
Act B : **Acton Bridge**	Edle : **Edleston**	Pick : **Pickmere**
And : **Anderton**	Elw : **Elworth**	Poole : **Poole**
Antr : **Antrobus**	Eng B : **Englesea Brook**	Rave : **Ravensmoor**
Arc : **Arclid**	Etti H : **Ettiley Heath**	Reas : **Reaseheath**
Arl : **Arley**	Gors : **Gorstage**	Rudh : **Rudheath**
Ast B : **Aston by Budworth**	Gt B : **Great Budworth**	Sandb : **Sandbach**
Ast M : **Aston Juxta Mondrum**	Hart : **Hartford**	Sandi : **Sandiway**
Aust : **Austerson**	Hasl : **Haslington**	Shav : **Shavington**
B'ley : **Baddiley**	Hass : **Hassall**	Soun : **Sound**
B'ton : **Baddington**	Henh : **Henhull**	Spro : **Sproston**
Balt : **Balterley**	High W : **Higher Whitley**	Stan : **Stanthorne**
Barn : **Barnton**	Holm C : **Holmes Chapel**	Stap : **Stapeley**
Basf : **Basford**	Hou : **Hough**	Tab : **Tabley**
Bath : **Batherton**	Kind : **Kinderton**	Warm : **Warmingham**
Bla : **Blakelow**	Lach D : **Lach Dennis**	Weav : **Weaverham**
Blet : **Bletchton**	Leig : **Leighton**	West : **Weston**
Bost : **Bostock**	Lit L : **Little Leigh**	What : **Whatcroft**
Brad G : **Bradfield Green**	L Gral : **Lostock Gralam**	Whee : **Wheelock**
Bradw : **Bradwall**	L Gre : **Lostock Green**	Whit : **Whitegate**
Brer : **Brereton**	Malk B : **Malkins Bank**	Will : **Willaston**
Budw H : **Budworth Heath**	Marb : **Marbury**	Wimb : **Wimboldsley**
Burl : **Burland**	Mars : **Marston**	Winc : **Wincham**
Byl : **Byley**	Mart : **Marton**	Winn : **Winnington**
Chor : **Chorlton**	Mead : **Meadowbank**	Wins : **Winsford**
Comb : **Comberbach**	Midd : **Middlewich**	Wint : **Winterley**
Cran : **Cranage**	Mins V : **Minshull Vernon**	Wist : **Wistaston**
Crewe : **Crewe**	Most : **Moston**	Wool : **Woolstanwood**
Crewe G : **Crewe Green**	Moul : **Moulton**	Worl : **Worleston**
Crow : **Crowton**	Nant : **Nantwich**	Wyb : **Wybunbury**
Cudd : **Cuddington**	Norl : **Norley**	
Darn : **Darnhall**	Nort : **Northwich**	

A

Abbey Cl. CW7: Wins 5F 23
  CW8: Whit 2C 18
Abbeydale Cl. CW2: West 5G 49
Abbey Flds. CW2: Wist 5D 40
Abbey La. CW8: Hart 2D 14
Abbey Pk. Way CW2: Eng B, West 4H 49
Abbey Pl. CW1: Crewe 5B 36
Abbey Rd. CW11: Sandb 3A 32
Abbey Way CW8: Hart 3D 14
Abbotsbury Cl. CW2: Wist 5H 41
Abbots Mere Cl. CW8: Sandi 5D 12
  (off Sandington Dr.)
Abbots Way CW8: Hart 3D 14
Abbotts Way CW7: Wins 1C 22
Aberfeldy Cl. CW4: Holm C 4D 28
Abington Cl. CW1: Crewe 5H 35
Acacia Cres. CW1: Crewe 5C 36
Acacia Dr. CW11: Sandb 2A 32
Acer Av. CW1: Crewe 4C 36
Acorn Bank Cl. CW2: Wist 6H 41
Acorn Cl. CW7: Wins 3A 24
  CW8: Cudd 5D 12
ACTON 6C 38
ACTON BRIDGE 2D 6
Acton Bridge Station (Rail) 3D 6
Acton La. CW8: Act B 2D 6
Acton Rd. CW2: Crewe 6D 34
Addison Cl. CW2: Wist 5F 41
Adelaide St. CW1: Crewe 6A 36
Adlington Dr. CW9: Nort 2A 16
  CW11: Sandb 2E 33
Adlington Rd. CW2: Crewe 2F 41
Agecroft Rd. CW9: Nort 6C 10
Ainsworth La. CW8: Crow 3A 6
Ainsworth Rd. CW8: Weav 4A 8
Aire Pl. CW7: Wins .2B 24
  (off Nun Ho. Dr.)
Aitchison Rd. CW9: L Gral 3G 11
Alamein Dr. CW7: Wins 3F 23
Alamein Rd. CW8: Barn 1B 8
Alan St. CW9: Nort .5B 10
Alban St. CW1: Crewe 6A 36
Albert Pl. CW9: Nort 5B 10
Albert St. CW1: Crewe 6A 36
  CW5: Nant 1G 45
Albion Rd. CW9: Nort 4A 10
Albion St. CW2: Crewe 2G 41
Alder Dr. CW1: Crewe 4F 35
Alderley Cl. CW11: Sandb 2F 33
Alderley Rd. CW8: Winn 5F 9
Alder Rd. CW8: Weav 5H 7
Aldersey Rd. CW2: Crewe 2F 41
Alderton Gro. CW7: Wins 5H 19
Aldford Cl. CW2: Hou 5C 48
Aldford Way CW7: Wins 1D 22
Aldington Dr. CW10: Midd 6B 26
Alexandra Pl. CW1: Crewe 6H 35
Alexandra Rd. CW10: Midd 5B 26
Alexandra Soccer Cen. 1A 48
Alexandra Sq. CW7: Wins 3C 22
  (off Brunner Pl.)
Alexandra Stadium 3B 42
Alexandra St. CW7: Wins 2E 23
Alford Ct. CW9: Nort 2G 15
  (off Harthill Cl.)
Alfred St. CW8: Nort 1G 15
Allen Dr. CW9: Dave 5H 15
Allen Pl. CW1: Crewe 6H 35
Allgreave Cl. CW10: Midd 5A 26
Allman Cl. CW1: Crewe 4F 35
Alma Av. CW1: Crewe 5A 36
Almond Av. CW1: Crewe 5B 36
Almond Gro. CW8: Weav 6A 8
Alton St. CW2: Crewe 2F 41
Alt Wlk. CW7: Wins .1A 24
Alumbrook Av. CW4: Holm C 3E 29
Alum Ct. CW4: Holm C 4E 29
Alundale Rd. CW7: Wins 6E 19
Alvanley Ri. CW9: Nort 1A 16
Alvaston Bus. Pk. CW5: Nant 5H 39
Alvaston Rd. CW5: Nant 2H 45
Alvaston Wlk. CW2: Crewe 3F 41
Alvingham Cl. CW9: Nort 5B 10

Ambleside Cl. CW2: Crewe 3E 41
  CW7: Wins 6E 19
Ambuscade Cl. CW1: Crewe 6C 36
Amy St. CW2: Crewe 2A 42
Anderson Cl. CW1: Crewe 1D 42
ANDERTON 2F 9
Anderton Boat Lift 2F 9
Anderton Boat Lift Vis Cen. 2F 9
Anderton Grange CW9: Nort 6H 9
Anderton Nature Pk. 2G 9
Angelina Cl. CW11: Elw 2H 31
Angus Gro. CW10: Midd 1B 26
Annions La. CW5: Stap, Wyb 6E 47
Ann St. CW9: Nort .4D 10
Anthony Dr. CW9: Moul 2H 19
Anvil Cl. CW11: Sandb 6B 32
Apollo Cinema
  Crewe 2B 42
Applefield CW8: Nort 6F 9
Apple Mkt. St. CW9: Nort 5H 9
Appleton St. CW8: Winn 4F 9
Arbour Cl. CW9: Nort 5C 10
Arderne Av. CW2: Crewe 3F 41
Ardleigh Cl. CW1: Crewe 3F 35
Arkwright Cl. CW7: Wins 3C 22
Arley Ct. CW9: Nort 2G 15
Arley Mossend La. CW9: Arl, Ast B 1D 4
Arley Pl. CW2: Wist .5G 41
Arley Rd. CW9: Nort 5C 10
Arley Wlk. CW11: Etti H 4H 31
Arlington Cl. CW2: Wist 5A 42
Armistead Way CW4: Cran 1C 28
Armitstead Rd. CW11: Sandb 5B 32
Arnold St. CW5: Nant 1G 45
Arnside Cl. CW7: Wins 1F 23
Arran Cl. CW4: Holm C 4E 29
Arran Pl. CW2: Crewe 2D 40
Arthur St. CW2: Crewe 3B 42
  CW9: L Gral 3G 11
Artle Rd. CW2: Crewe 5A 42
Arundel Cl. CW2: Wist 5E 41
Ashbank CW9: Rudh 6D 10
Ashbourne Dr. CW2: West 5G 49
Ashby Dr. CW11: Etti H 4G 31
Ash Cl. CW4: Holm C 2F 29
Ashcroft Av. CW2: Shav 4H 47
Ashfield St. CW10: Midd 3B 26
Ashgate La. CW9: Winc 5F 5
Ash Gro. CW5: Nant 3G 45
  CW7: Wins 3F 23
  CW8: Weav 6A 8
  CW10: Midd 4B 26
Ash Ho. CW11: Sandb 3E 33
Ash Ho. La. CW8: Lit L 4A 2
Ashlea Dr. CW5: Will 2E 47
Ashley Dr. CW8: Hart 1C 14
Ashley Grange CW9: Dave 4G 15
Ashley Mdw. CW1: Hasl 6H 37
Ashmore Cl. CW10: Midd 5A 26
Ashmuir Cl. CW1: Crewe 5H 35
Ash Rd. CW1: Crewe 5B 36
  CW8: Sandi 5D 12
Ash St. CW9: Nort .4A 10
Ashton Cl. CW9: Nort 3G 15
  CW10: Midd 6B 26
Ashville Ct. CW2: Wist 6H 41
Ashwood Cl. CW8: Barn 1D 8
Ashwood Cres. CW8: Barn 2D 8
Ash Wood Pk. CW9: Winc 2C 10
Aspens, The CW8: Cudd 2B 12
Asquith Cl. CW1: Hasl 6G 37
Astbury Cl. CW1: Crewe 4G 35
Astbury Dr. CW8: Barn 1C 8
Astle Cl. CW10: Midd 4A 26
Aston Av. CW7: Wins 1D 22
Aston Way CW10: Midd 2C 26
Athelbrae Cl. CW8: Nort 6H 9
Atholl Av. CW2: Crewe 4A 42
Atholl Cl. CW1: Hasl 1G 43
Audlem Dr. CW9: Nort 2A 16
Audlem Rd. CW5: Nant 4G 45
Audley St. CW1: Crewe 3B 42
  (not continuous)
Audley St. W. CW1: Crewe 6B 36
Austen Cl. CW11: Elw 3H 31
Austin Cl. CW7: Wins 5E 23
Austin St. CW9: Nort 3D 10

Avenue, The CW9: Comb 3F 3
  CW9: Gt B .3B 4
  CW9: Mars 2B 10
  CW11: Elw 1A 32
Avenue Engineering Pk. CW8: Winn 5E 9
Avenue One CW1: Crewe 4G 43
Avenue Two CW1: Crewe 5H 43
Avocet Dr. CW7: Wins 5F 23
Avon Dr. CW1: Crewe 6E 37
Avon Wlk. CW7: Wins 1A 24
Ayrshire Cl. CW10: Midd 1B 26
Aysgarth Av. CW1: Leig 2H 35

B

Bachelors Wing, The CW10: Bost 4D 20
Backlands CW1: Crewe 5A 36
Back La. CW2: Shav 2C 48
Baddiley Cl. CW5: B'ley 5A 44
Baddiley La. CW5: B'ley, Rave 6A 44
Baddington La. CW5: B'ton 6E 45
Badger Av. CW1: Crewe 5F 35
Badger Cl. CW9: Nort 2C 22
Badgers Set CW8: Cudd 2B 12
Badgers Wood CW2: Wist 5E 41
Bag La. CW8: Crow, Cudd 1A 12
  WA6: Norl .1A 12
Bagmere Cl. CW11: Sandb 2A 32
Bailey Cl. CW1: Crewe 4A 36
Bailey Cres. CW11: Sandb 3F 33
Baker Cl. CW2: Crewe 3G 41
Baker's Ct. CW7: Wins 1G 23
Baker's La. CW7: Wins 1G 23
Balfour Cl. CW1: Hasl 1G 43
Balmoral Av. CW2: Crewe 4H 41
  CW9: Nort 2A 16
Balmoral Cl. CW7: Wins 6E 19
Balmoral Dr. CW4: Holm C 4D 28
Balmoral Pl. CW2: Will 3D 46
Bancroft CW8: Act B 1C 6
Bankfield Av. CW2: Wist 6G 41
Bank Ho. CW7: Wins 2E 23
Bank La. CW5: Burl .5A 38
Bankside CW8: Weav 4G 7
Bank Top Cotts. CW5: Nant 1H 45
  (off Birchin La.)
Bannacks Cl. CW5: Will 1D 46
Bannister Gro. CW7: Wins 5D 22
Barber's La. CW8: Nort 5G 9
  CW5: Nant 2G 45
Barker St. CW2: Crewe 4B 42
Barleywood Cl. CW2: Wist 5H 41
Barlow Dr. CW7: Wins 3B 22
Barlow Rd. CW9: Moul 2G 19
Barlow Way CW11: Sandb 1C 32
Barnabas Av. CW1: Crewe 6F 35
Barnato Cl. CW1: Crewe 4F 35
Barnbrook Cl. CW7: Wins 2C 22
Barnes Cl. CW1: Hasl 1H 43
Barnett Wlk. CW2: Crewe 5A 42
  (off Brookhouse Dr.)
Barn Mdw. CW8: Winn 4F 9
Barns, The CW10: Bost 4D 20
Barnside Way CW8: Moul 1H 19
BARNTON 2D 8
Barnwell Cl. CW2: Wist 5H 41
Baronia Pl. CW5: Nant 1H 45
Barons Quay CW9: Nort 4H 9
Barons Quay Rd. CW9: Nort 4H 9
Barons Rd. CW2: Shav 3H 47
  CW5: Poole, Worl 1H 39
BARONY, THE 1H 45
Barony Bldgs. CW5: Nant 1G 45
Barony Ct. CW5: Nant 6G 39
Barony Employment Pk., The
  CW5: Nant 6H 39
Barony Rd. CW5: Nant 6G 39
Barony Sports Complex 1H 45
Barony Ter. CW5: Nant 1G 45
Barracks La. CW5: Rave 6A 44
Barrastitch La. CW8: Cudd 2C 12
Barrie Gro. CW1: Crewe 1C 42
Barrington Dr. CW10: Midd 4A 26
Barrows Cl. CW1: Crewe 3G 35
BARROWS GREEN 3F 35
Barrymore Cres. CW9: Comb 3F 3

Barrymore Rd.—Briardale Cl.

Barrymore Rd. CW8: Weav 4A **8**
Barthomley Cres. CW2: Crewe 1D **40**
Barton Ct. CW7: Wins 2H **23**
Bartons Pl. CW9: Nort 4B **10**
Basford Rd. CW2: Crewe 5B **42**
Basford Way CW7: Wins 1D **22**
Basset Cl. CW5: Will 1D **46**
Bateman Cl. CW1: Crewe 1H **41**
Bateman Rd. CW9: L Gral 3H **11**
Batemans Ct. CW2: Wist 5H **41**
Batherton La. CW5: Bath, Nant 5H **45**
Bath St. CW11: Sandb 3E **33**
Batterbee Ct. CW1: Hasl 6H **37**
Bayley Rd. CW5: Will 2D **46**
Beach Gro. CW8: Hart 1E **15**
Beach Rd. CW8: Hart 1C **14**
Beagle Point CW7: Wins 2C **22**
Beames Ho. *CW1: Crewe 1H* ***41***
(off Harrison Rd.)
Beam Heath Way CW5: Nant 6H **39**
Beam St. CW5: Nant 1G **45**
Beatty Rd. CW5: Nant 3F **45**
Beaulieu Av. CW7: Wins 1H **23**
Beaumont Cl. CW2: Wist 5F **41**
Beauty Bank CW8: Whit 4A **18**
Beaver Cen., The CW9: Nort 6H **9**
Beaver Cl. WA16: Pick 4F **5**
Becconsall Cl. CW1: Crewe 3G **35**
Becconsall Dr. CW1: Crewe 3G **35**
Beckenham Gro. CW7: Wins 2C **22**
Beckett Av. CW7: Wins 3D **24**
Beckford Cl. CW1: Crewe 3F **35**
Bedford Ct. CW2: Crewe 4B **42**
Bedford Gdns. CW2: Crewe 4A **42**
Bedford Pl. CW2: Crewe 4A **42**
Bedford Ri. CW7: Wins 5E **23**
Bedford St. CW2: Crewe 4A **42**
Beech Cl. CW4: Holm C 2F **29**
CW8: Cudd 5D **12**
Beechcroft Av. CW2: Wist 6H **41**
Beech Dr. CW2: Crewe 3E **41**
Beeches, The CW5: Nant 2G **45**
Beechfield CW9: Moul 1G **19**
Beechfield Dr. CW10: Midd 1H **25**
Beechfield Gdns. CW8: Hart 1D **14**
Beechfields CW7: Wins 3B **24**
Beech Gro. CW1: Crewe 6C **36**
CW7: Wins 4F **23**
CW8: Weav 5H **7**
CW11: Sandb 3F **33**
Beech Heyes Cl. CW8: Weav 5A **8**
Beech Heyes Dr. CW8: Weav 6A **8**
Beech La. CW8: Barn 2C **8**
Beech Ri. CW8: Crow 3A **6**
Beech St. CW1: Crewe 1A **42**
CW10: Midd 2A **26**
Beech Tree Cl. CW5: Will 2D **46**
Beechwood Av. CW8: Hart 1C **14**
Beechwood Cl. CW5: Stap 3A **46**
Beechwood Dr. CW9: Winc 5F **5**
Beehive La. CW9: Moul 6H **15**
Beeston Cl. CW4: Holm C 3C **28**
CW10: Midd 6B **26**
Beeston Dr. CW7: Wins 4E **23**
Beeston St. CW8: Nort 6G **9**
Belgrave Rd. CW2: Crewe 3H **41**
CW9: Nort 3A **16**
Belgravia Ct. *CW8: Hart 2E* ***15***
(off Sandringham Pl.)
Belle Vue Ter. CW11: Sandb 3D **32**
Belmont Av. CW11: Sandb 2C **32**
Belmont Rd. CW9: Budw H, Gt B 3H **3**
CW9: Nort 6C **10**
Beltony Dr. CW1: Leig 2G **35**
Bembridge Ct. CW10: Midd 3A **26**
Bembridge Dr. CW10: Midd 3A **26**
Benjafield Ct. CW1: Crewe 4F **35**
Bennett Cl. CW1: Crewe 1C **42**
Bennett Ct. CW7: Wins 6F **23**
Bennett Rd. CW9: Rudh 1D **16**
Bent La. CW8: Crow 4A **6**
Bentley Dr. CW1: Crewe 6E **37**
Bentley Gro. CW7: Wins 5E **23**
Berkeley Cres. CW2: Wist 5G **41**
Berkeley Ri. CW7: Wins 3C **22**
Berrystead CW8: Hart 3D **14**
Berwick Ct. CW4: Holm C 4D **28**
Bessancourt CW4: Holm C 3E **29**
Beswick Dr. CW1: Crewe 2E **43**
Beswicks Rd. CW8: Nort 4G **9**
Betchton Cl. CW11: Sandb 2E **33**
BETCHTON HEATH 4G **33**
Betchton Rd. CW11: Blet, Malk B 6E **33**
Betchton Vs. Cvn. Pk. CW11: Blet 4G **33**
Betjeman Way CW1: Crewe 6D **36**
Betley Cl. CW9: Nort 2A **16**
Betley St. CW1: Crewe 1A **42**
Bexington Dr. CW1: Crewe 3H **35**
Bexton Av. CW7: Wins 1C **22**
Bickerton Way CW9: Nort 3G **15**
Bickley Cl. CW2: Hou 5C **48**
CW9: Nort 2G **15**
Bidvale Way CW1: Crewe 4B **36**
BILLINGE GREEN 4D **16**
Billington Cl. CW2: Crewe 3G **41**
CW8: Barn 2B **8**
Bilton Way CW2: Crewe 6E **35**
Binney Rd. CW9: Nort 5B **10**
Binyon Way CW1: Crewe 1E **43**
Birchall Ct. CW5: Nant 3H **45**
Birchall Wlk. CW2: Crewe 5B **42**
Birch Av. CW1: Crewe 6D **36**
CW7: Wins 2A **24**
Birch Cl. CW1: Crewe 6D **36**
CW4: Holm C 3F **29**
Birches, The CW2: Crewe 5A **42**
Birches La. CW9: Lach D, L Gre 4G **11**
Birch Gdns. CW11: Sandb 4E **33**
Birch Gro. CW9: L Gre 6H **11**
CW9: Winc 6F **5**
Birchin Cl. CW5: Nant 1A **46**
Birchin La. CW5: Nant 1H **45**
Birch La. CW2: Hou 5D **48**
CW10: Stan 1F **25**
Birchmuir Cl. CW1: Crewe 5H **35**
Birchwood Dr. CW5: Nant 1H **45**
Birkdale Ct. CW9: Nort 5B **10**
Birkdale Gdns. CW7: Wins 1C **22**
Birkenhead St. CW9: Nort 5C **10**
Birtles Cl. CW11: Sandb 2E **33**
Birtwistle Rd. CW9: Rudh 1D **16**
Bishopgates Dr. CW9: Nort 3G **15**
Bishops Wood CW5: Nant 4H **45**
Blackacres Cl. CW11: Sandb 3B **32**
Blackcroft Av. CW8: Barn 3C **8**
Blackthorn Cl. CW2: Wist 5H **41**
Blackwell Cl. CW10: Midd 5B **26**
Blagg Av. CW5: Nant 3E **45**
Blake Cl. CW2: Wist 4F **41**
Blakeden La. CW7: Wins 1A **22**
Blake La. CW8: Sandi 5E **13**
BLAKELOW 3E **47**
Blakelow Cl. CW10: Midd 4H **25**
Blakelow Cres. CW5: Bla 4F **47**
Blakelow Dr. CW5: Will 3D **46**
Blakemere Craft Cen. 6D **12**
Blakemere Dr. CW9: Nort 2G **15**
Blakemere Way CW11: Sandb 1B **32**
Blandford Dr. CW9: Nort 4G **15**
Blankney, The CW5: Nant 3G **45**
Bleasdale Rd. CW1: Leig 2H **35**
Blenheim Cl. CW2: Wist 5E **41**
CW9: Nort 3H **15**
Blenheim Gdns. CW7: Wins 4E **23**
Blenheim Pk. CW11: Sandb 5C **32**
Blossom Hgts. CW8: Nort 6F **9**
Blount Cl. CW1: Crewe 1H **41**
Bluebell Cl. CW8: Nort 4G **9**
Blunstone Cl. CW2: Crewe 3G **41**
Blythe Pl. *CW7: Wins 2B* ***24***
(off Nun Ho. Dr.)
Boardmans Pl. CW9: Nort 2H **15**
Boden Dr. CW5: Will 3D **46**
Bodnant Cl. CW1: Crewe 3G **35**
Bold St. CW1: Hasl 1G **43**
CW11: Sandb 3D **32**
Bollands Row *CW5: Nant 2G* ***45***
(off Churche's Ct.)
Bollin Av. CW7: Wins 1B **24**
Bollin Cl. CW7: Wins 1B **24**
CW11: Sandb 2A **32**
Bollington Av. CW9: Nort 1A **16**
Bolshaw Cl. CW1: Crewe 4G **35**
Bond St. CW8: Winn 4F **9**
Booth Av. CW11: Sandb 3E **33**
Booth Hall CW1: Crewe 2E **43**
Booth La. CW10: Midd, Most 3B **26**
CW11: Most, Sandb 1G **31**
Booth Rd. CW8: Hart 3C **14**
Boothsmere Cl. CW11: Sandb 1B **32**
Borrowdale Cl. CW2: Crewe 2E **41**
Bosley Cl. CW10: Midd 5A **26**
BOSTOCK GREEN 2B **20**
Bostock Rd. CW7: Wins 5A **20**
CW10: Bost, Stan 4B **20**
Boulton Cl. CW11: Malk B 6E **33**
Boundary La. Nth. CW8: Cudd 5D **12**
Boundary La. Sth. CW8: Cudd 5D **12**
Boundary St. CW9: Nort 3E **11**
Bourne Cl. CW8: Weav 6A **8**
Bowden Dr. CW9: Nort 5C **10**
Bowen Cooke Av. CW1: Crewe 5G **35**
Bowen St. CW2: Crewe 2G **41**
Bowers Row CW5: Nant 2G **45**
Bowland Cft. CW1: Leig 2H **35**
Bowland Ri. CW7: Wins 4D **22**
Bowles Cl. CW11: Sandb 3C **32**
Bowline Cl. CW11: Malk B 6F **33**
Bowling Grn. Ct. *CW5: Nant 2G* ***45***
(off The Gullet)
CW8: Nort 4G **9**
Bowmere Dr. CW7: Wins 3E **23**
Bowness Av. CW7: Wins 1F **23**
Bowness Cl. CW4: Holm C 3C **28**
Bowness Rd. CW2: Crewe 2D **40**
Bowyer Av. CW5: Nant 1G **45**
Brackenfield Way CW7: Wins 3C **22**
Bracken Way CW8: Barn 2D **8**
CW9: Comb 4E **3**
CW9: Winc 2C ***10***
(off Hawthorn Wlk.)
Brackenwood Cl. CW2: Wist 5H **41**
Brackenwood M. CW2: West 5H **49**
Bradburns La. CW8: Hart 1D **14**
Bradbury Rd. CW7: Wins 6A **20**
Bradburys La. *WA16: Pick 4F* ***5***
(off Park La.)
Braddon Cl. CW9: Dave 3H **15**
Bradeley Hall Rd. CW1: Crewe, Hasl 6E **37**
Bradeley Rd. CW1: Crewe 6E **37**
CW1: Hasl 1G **43**
BRADFIELD GREEN 1E **35**
Bradfield Rd. CW1: Crewe 3F **35**
Bradford Rd. CW7: Mead, Wins 3F **19**
BRADFORD WOOD 5E **19**
Bradley Cl. CW10: Midd 4H **25**
Bradwall Rd. CW10: Kind, Midd 4E **27**
CW11: Sandb 1D **32**
Bradwall St. CW11: Sandb 2D **32**
Braemar Av. CW9: Nort 6C **10**
Braemar Cl. CW2: Wist 5E **41**
CW4: Holm C 4E **29**
Brakeley La. CW8: Lit L 1H **7**
Bramall Cl. CW11: Sandb 2E **33**
Bramble Cl. CW7: Wins 6E **19**
CW10: Midd 1C **26**
Brambles, The CW1: Hasl 1F **43**
CW9: Winc 2C **10**
Brambles Chase CW8: Cudd 5D **12**
Bramhall Cl. CW7: Wins 2D **22**
Bramhall Ct. CW2: Crewe 3F **41**
Bramhall Dr. CW4: Holm C 3C **28**
Bramhall Rd. CW2: Crewe 3F **41**
CW4: Holm C 3C **28**
Bramhalls Pk. CW9: And 2E **9**
Brampton Cl. CW2: Eng B 4H **49**
Brassey Ct. CW5: Will 1C **46**
Brassey Way CW5: Will 2D **46**
Bratt's La. CW8: Cudd 2A **12**
WA6: Norl 2A **12**
Bray Cl. CW1: Crewe 6C **36**
Brecon Way CW2: Wist 6G **41**
CW7: Wins 3D **22**
Brereton Cl. CW2: Crewe 3E **41**
CW11: Sandb 2E **33**
Brereton Dr. CW5: Nant 1H **45**
Brereton La. CW4: Spro 1G **27**
CW10: Midd 1G **27**
CW11: Brer 1G **27**
Brereton Rd. CW8: Hart 3C **14**
Briardale Cl. CW2: Wist 5F **41**

52 A-Z Crewe

Briar La. CW8: Weav 6A 8
Briarwood Ct. CW7: Wins 3E 23
Brick Bank CW5: Nant 2H 45
Brickfield Bus. Cen. CW9: Nort 4D 10
Brick Kiln La. CW10: Bost 2B 20
Brickley Ct. CW8: Weav 4G 7
(off Chapel St.)
Bridge Cl. CW2: Wist 6G 41
CW8: Cudd 4E 13
Bridge La. CW8: Cudd 4D 12
Bridgemere Cl. CW11: Sandb 1B 32
Bridgemere Way CW9: Nort 3G 15
Bridge St. CW9: Nort 3E 11
Bridle Hey CW5: Nant 5H 45
Bridle Rd. CW2: Crewe 2H 41
Brierley Bus. Cen. CW1: Crewe 1B 42
Brierley Ct. CW7: Wins 3H 23
Brierley St. CW1: Crewe 1B 42
Briggs Av. CW2: Crewe 4B 42
Bright St. CW1: Crewe 1H 41
Brindley Av. CW7: Wins 2E 23
Brindley Pk. CW11: Sandb 6B 32
Brine Rd. CW5: Nant 4G 45
Britannia Dr. CW9: Rudh 1E 17
Broadacre CW9: Comb 5F 3
Broad La. CW4: Spro 3H 27
CW5: Bath, Stap 5A 46
Broadleigh Way CW2: Crewe 5A 42
Broad St. CW1: Crewe 6A 36
Broadway CW8: Barn 2D 8
Broadway, The CW5: Nant 2H 45
Broady Ct. CW2: Crewe 3A 42
Brock Hollow CW11: Sandb 5B 32
Brockhurst M. CW9: Nort 1A 16
Brockhurst St. CW9: Nort 5A 10
Brockhurst Way CW9: Nort 1A 16
Brocklebank Dr. CW8: Nort 6G 9
Brockwell Cl. CW7: Wins 3C 22
BROKEN CROSS 1E 17
Broken Cross Pl. CW9: Rudh 6E 11
Bromley Cl. CW1: Crewe 3F 35
Bromley Dr. CW4: Holm C 4E 29
Brook Av. CW2: Shav 2A 48
Brook Cl. CW1: Crewe 2D 42
Brook Ct. CW11: Sandb 3D 32
Brookdale Pk. CW2: Crewe 2G 41
Brookfield CW1: Hasl 6H 37
Brookfield Ct. CW1: Crewe 6H 35
Brookfield Dr. CW4: Holm C 3D 28
Brookfield Pk. CW5: Nant 3G 45
Brookfield Rd. CW9: Comb 3F 3
Brookhouse Dr. CW2: Crewe 4A 42
Brookhouse Rd. CW11: Sandb 3D 32
Brookland Av. CW2: Wist 5F 41
Brookland Dr. CW11: Sandb 3F 33
Brooklands CW1: Crewe 6A 36
Brooklands, The CW2: Hou 4C 48
Brooklands Dr. CW9: Nort 3A 16
Brooklands Gro. CW1: Crewe 5G 35
Brooklands Ho. CW1: Crewe 5H 35
Brook La. CW9: Nort 6D 10
Brooklyn St. CW2: Crewe 3A 42
Brookmere Cl. CW11: Sandb 1A 32
Brook Side CW8: Weav 4G 7
Brookside CW8: Cudd 4D 12
Brookside Grn. CW2: Crewe 5A 42
(off Artle Rd.)
Brooks La. CW10: Midd 2B 26
Brooks La. Ind. Est. CW10: Midd 2B 26
(not continuous)
Brook St. CW2: Crewe 2B 42
CW9: Nort 3E 11
(Victoria St.)
CW9: Nort 4A 10
(Witton St.)
Brook Ter. CW11: Sandb 6C 32
Brookview CW2: Wist 5A 42
Brook Way CW5: Nant 4G 45
CW8: Hart 3D 14
(off Riddings La.)
Broomfield Cl. CW7: Wins 3C 22
Broomfield La. CW8: Barn 1B 8
Broom St. CW1: Crewe 6G 35
Broughton La. CW2: Wist 4F 41
Broughton Rd. CW1: Crewe 2A 36
Brown Av. CW5: Nant 4H 45
Browning Cl. CW11: Etti H 4H 31

Browning St. CW1: Crewe 1A 42
Browning Way CW7: Wins 4B 22
Brownlees Cl. CW2: Crewe 4G 41
Broxton Av. CW10: Midd 5B 26
Brunel Ct. CW9: Rudh 2D 16
Brunner Gro. CW5: Nant 2A 46
Brunner Pl. CW7: Wins 3C 22
Brynlow Dr. CW10: Midd 3H 25
Buchan Gro. CW2: Crewe 2H 41
Buckfast Way CW10: Midd 2H 25
Buckingham Cl. CW2: Wist 5E 41
Buckingham Dr. CW7: Wins 4E 23
CW9: Nort 3G 15
Buck Cl. CW2: Hou 4C 48
Buckley Cl. CW10: Midd 3H 25
Bude Cl. CW1: Crewe 3H 35
Budworth Cl. CW11: Sandb 2A 32
Budworth Heath La. CW9: Ast B, Budw H . . .2B 4
Budworth La. CW9: Comb, Gt B 4F 3
Budworth Rd. CW9: Arl, Ast B 2C 4
CW9: Ast B, Pick, Tab 1G 5
WA16: Pick, Tab 1G 5
Budworth Sailing Club 4A 4
Bulkeley St. CW1: Crewe 2C 42
Bull Ring CW9: Nort 5H 9
(off Watling St.)
Bullring, The CW10: Midd 2A 26
Bunbury Cl. CW9: Nort 2A 16
CW10: Midd 6B 26
BURFORD 5B 38
Burgamot La. CW9: Comb 3F 3
Burgess Cl. CW5: Stap 3B 46
Burgess La. WA6: Norl 2A 12
Burgess Pl. CW8: Nort 5G 9
(off Ryders St.)
Burjen Way CW1: Crewe 5H 35
Burland Gro. CW7: Wins 1C 22
Burlea Cl. CW2: Crewe 6E 35
Burlea Dr. CW2: Shav 2H 47
Burnell Cl. CW5: Nant 4H 45
Burns Dr. CW1: Crewe 1D 42
Burnside Way CW8: Winn 4F 9
Burrows, The CW8: Cudd 2B 12
Burrows Hill CW8: Nort 6D 8
Burton Gro. CW1: Leig 2H 35
Burwardsley Way CW9: Nort 3G 15
Butley Cl. CW10: Midd 5A 26
Buttercup Way WA16: Pick 5F 5
Buttermere Dr. CW1: Leig 2H 35
Buttermere Rd. CW7: Wins 1E 23
BUTT GREEN .4B 46
Buxton Av. CW1: Crewe 1C 42
Byley La. CW4: Cran 1B 28
CW10: Cran 1A 28
CW10: Midd 1C 26
Byley Way CW7: Wins 2D 22
Byron Cl. CW1: Crewe 1D 42
CW10: Midd 6B 26
CW11: Etti H 3H 31
Byron Wlk. CW5: Nant 1F 45
Byron Way CW2: Wist 4F 41

C

Caerleon Cl. CW7: Wins 3C 22
Caernarvon Av. CW7: Wins 4D 22
Caernarvon Rd. CW2: Wist 5E 41
Caister Way CW7: Wins 4E 23
Calder Av. CW1: Crewe 6E 37
Caldicott Cl. CW7: Wins 4E 23
Caldwell Cl. CW5: Stap 3B 46
Caldy Way CW7: Wins 2D 22
Calveley Cl. CW9: Nort 2G 15
Calveley Way CW7: Wins 2D 22
(off Woodcott Av.)
Cambrian Way CW7: Wins 3D 22
Cambridge Av. CW7: Wins 2C 22
Camden St. CW1: Crewe 1B 42
(off Earle St.)
Camelot Gro. CW2: Shav 3A 48
Cameron Av. CW2: Shav 4H 47
Camm St. CW2: Crewe 3B 42
Camomile La. CW8: Cudd 2A 12
Campbell Cl. CW1: Hasl 1G 43
CW9: Nort 3H 15

Canal Side CW8: Barn 3D 8
Canal Ter. CW10: Midd 3B 26
Canford Cl. CW1: Crewe 3H 35
Canton Pl. CW8: Nort 6F 9
Capel Way CW5: Nant 1F 45
Capenhurst Av. CW2: Crewe 2F 41
Capesthorne Cl. CW4: Holm C 3D 28
CW9: Nort 3H 15
CW11: Sandb 2E 33
Capesthorne Rd. CW2: Crewe 3E 41
Carden Av. CW7: Wins 2D 22
Carisbrook Dr. CW7: Wins 4E 23
Carisbrooke Cl. CW2: Wist 5E 41
Carlisle Cl. CW7: Wins 2C 22
Carlisle St. CW2: Crewe 3H 41
Carlton Rd. CW9: Nort 6A 10
Carmarthen Cl. CW7: Wins 4E 23
Carnoustie Cl. CW7: Wins 1C 22
Carriage Dr. CW8: Hart 2E 15
Carrington Way CW1: Crewe 3H 35
Carroll Dr. CW2: Wist 5F 41
Carter Cl. CW5: Nant 1F 45
Cartlake Cl. CW5: Nant 2E 45
Cartledge Cl. CW8: Cudd 4E 13
Cartmel Cl. CW4: Holm C 3C 28
CW7: Wins 1F 23
Cartwright Rd. CW1: Hasl 6H 37
Carver Cl. CW7: Wins 5A 20
Casey La. CW2: Basf, Chor, Shav 4D 48
CASSIA GREEN 4A 18
Cassia Grn. La. CW7: Mart 4A 18
Cassia La. CW7: Mart 4A 18
Casson St. CW1: Crewe 6H 35
Castle Bank CW8: Nort 6G 9
Castle Cliff CW8: Nort 6G 9
(off Waterloo Rd.)
Castle Cl. CW8: Nort 6G 9
Castlemead Wlk. CW9: Nort 3G 15
Castlemere Dr. CW1: Crewe 4A 36
Castle St. CW1: Crewe 1A 42
CW5: Nant 2G 45
CW8: Nort 5G 9
Catalan Cl. CW7: Wins 2A 24
Catherine St. CW2: Crewe 3B 42
Cavendish Cl. CW7: Wins 3C 22
Cavendish Rd. CW2: Crewe 6E 35
Cavendish Way CW4: Holm C 3C 28
Cecil Rigby Cl. CW11: Sandb 3D 32
Cedar Cl. CW4: Holm C 2F 29
CW9: L Gral 2G 11
CW10: Midd 5C 26
CW11: Sandb 4E 33
Cedar Ct. CW5: Will 1D 46
Cedar Dr. CW8: Barn 1C 8
Cedar Gro. CW5: Nant 2A 46
CW7: Wins 2A 24
Cedar Rd. CW8: Weav 5G 7
Cedars, The CW5: Nant 2F 45
Cedar Way CW2: Wist 6H 41
Cedarwood CW8: Cudd 3B 12
Cemetery Rd. CW2: West 2F 49
Central Dr. CW8: Barn 2C 8
Central Gro. CW9: Rudh 1D 16
Central Rd. CW9: Rudh 6D 10
Centurion Way CW10: Midd 1B 26
Cestria Cl. CW11: Elw 2H 31
Chads Grn. CW5: Wyb 6G 47
Chadwell Ct. CW2: Eng B 3H 49
(off Abbey Pk. Way)
Chadwick Ct. CW10: Midd 4B 26
Chadwicke Cl. CW5: Stap 3H 45
Chadwick Flds. Orchard CW10: Midd 5B 26
(off Coronation Rd.)
Chadwick Rd. CW10: Midd 5A 26
Chaffinch Way CW7: Wins 5F 23
Chalfield Cl. CW2: Wist 6H 41
Chalfont Cres. CW2: West 5F 49
Chamberlain Dr. CW1: Hasl 6G 37
Chambers St. CW2: Crewe 3B 42
Chantry Av. CW8: Hart 3D 14
Chantry Ct. CW1: Crewe 1B 42
Chapel Cl. CW9: Comb 4F 3
Chapel Ct. CW9: Nort 6H 9
Chapel La. CW1: Crewe 2B 36
CW5: B'ley 5A 44
CW8: Act B 2B 6
CW9: Moul 1G 19

Chapelmere Cl. CW11: Sandb 2A 32
Chapelmere Ct. CW1: Crewe 4A 36
Chapel M. CW5: Nant 2G 45
    (off Market St.)
Chapel Rd. CW7: Wins 1H 23
Chapel Row CW5: Nant 2F 45
    (off Welsh Row)
Chapel St. CW2: Crewe 2B 42
  CW8: Nort 6G 9
    (not continuous)
  CW8: Weav 4G 7
  CW9: Moul 1G 19
  CW9: Winc 2C 10
  CW11: Sandb 3D 32
  CW11: Whee 6C 32
Charlcote Cres. CW2: Crewe 5A 42
Charles Av. CW9: Dave 5H 15
Charles St. CW1: Crewe 1A 42
Charlesworth Ct. CW11: Sandb 3E 33
Charlesworth St. CW1: Crewe 5B 36
Chartley Gro. CW10: Midd 1B 26
Chartwell Gro. CW7: Wins 6E 23
Chartwell Pk. CW11: Sandb 5C 32
Chassagne Sq. CW1: Crewe 4F 35
    (off Alder Rd.)
Chater Dr. CW5: Nant 4H 45
Chatham Way CW1: Hasl 6G 37
Chatsworth Cl. CW2: Wist 5G 41
  CW9: Nort 2A 16
Chaucer Gro. CW11: Etti H 4G 31
Cheerbrook Rd. CW5: Will 3C 46
Cheese Hill La. CW8: Cudd, Oak 2H 11
Chelford Dr. CW9: Nort 2H 15
Chell St. CW1: Crewe 6H 35
Cheltenham Cres. CW1: Crewe 4H 35
Chepstow Cl. CW7: Wins 4E 23
Cheriton Way CW2: Wist 5G 41
Cherrington Rd. CW5: Nant 4G 45
Cherry Cres. CW7: Wins 3E 23
Cherry Gro. CW5: Nant 2F 45
Cherry La. CW8: Cudd 5D 12
  CW8: Weav 5H 7
Cherry Tree Av. CW8: Barn 1C 8
Cherry Tree Ct. CW5: Stap 3A 46
Cherry Tree Rd. CW1: Crewe 5B 36
Cherrywood Cres. CW8: Barn 2D 8
Cheryl Ct. CW8: Cudd 3B 12
Cheshire Academy of Integrated Sports & Arts
  . . . . .2C 42
Chester Bri. CW2: Crewe 1A 42
    (off Edleston Rd.)
Chesterfield Cl. CW7: Wins 2B 22
Chester La. CW7: Wins 1A 22
Chester Rd. CW4: Holm C 3C 28
  CW5: Act 5B 38
  CW7: Wins 1B 22
  CW8: Hart, Nort, Sandi 4H 13
  CW8: Oak, Sandi 6A 12
  CW10: Midd 1G 26
Chester Sq. CW1: Crewe 1A 42
Chester St. CW1: Crewe 1A 42
Chesterton Cl. CW10: Midd 6C 26
Chesterton Dr. CW2: Wist 4F 41
Chesterton Gro. CW11: Etti H 4H 31
Chesterton Way CW2: Eng B 4H 49
Chester Way CW8: Nort 5H 9
  CW9: Nort 5A 10
Chestnut Av. CW2: Shav 2A 48
Chestnut Cl. CW8: Cudd 5D 12
  CW10: Midd 1H 25
Chestnut Dr. CW4: Holm C 3F 29
Chestnut Gro. CW1: Crewe 1C 42
  CW7: Wins 3E 23
  CW8: Barn 1D 8
Chetwode St. CW1: Crewe 6A 36
Cheviot Ct. CW7: Wins 4D 22
Cheviot Sq. CW7: Wins 4D 22
Cheyne Wlk. CW5: Nant 4G 45
Cheyney Wlk. CW2: Crewe 5A 42
Chidlow Cl. CW2: Hou 4C 48
Chilham Cl. CW7: Wins 4E 23
Chillingham Cl. CW10: Midd 4D 26
Chiltern Cl. CW2: West 6F 49
  CW8: Sandi .5E 13
Chiltern Way CW7: Wins 4D 22
Chilworth Cl. CW2: Crewe 5A 42
Chines, The CW8: Cudd 2B 12

Chipstead Cl. CW8: Hart 3C 14
Chirk Pl. CW7: Wins 2C 22
CHORLTON 5F 49
Chorlton La. CW2: Chor 6F 49
Christchurch Av. CW2: Crewe 4G 41
Christleton Av. CW2: Crewe 6D 34
  CW9: Nort 3A 16
Church Cl. CW8: Weav 4H 7
Churche's Ct. CW1: Nant 2G 45
Churchfields CW5: Wyb 6H 47
  CW8: Barn 2D 8
  CW8: Sandi .5F 13
CHURCH HILL .5F 23
Churchill Parkway CW7: Wins 3F 23
Church La. CW2: Wist 6E 41
  CW5: Nant 2G 45
  CW8: Weav 4H 7
  CW11: Sandb 1G 33
Church Mdws. CW8: Lit L 1H 7
Churchmere Dr. CW1: Crewe 4A 36
Church Ri. CW8: Sandi 5F 13
Church Rd. CW8: Barn 2D 8
  CW8: Lit L 1H 7
  CW8: Nort 4A 10
Churchside Cl. CW1: Hasl 6H 37
Church St. CW7: Wins 2G 23
  CW8: Weav 4H 7
    (off Church La.)
  CW8: Weav 4G 7
    (Northwich Rd.)
  CW9: Dave 4A 16
  CW9: Gt B 3A 4
  CW9: Moul 1H 19
  CW9: Winc 1E 11
  CW11: Sandb 3E 33
Church Vw. CW1: Hasl 6H 37
  CW4: Holm C 3E 29
    (off London Rd.)
Church Vw. Wlk. CW2: Wist 5E 41
    (off Rectory Cl.)
Church Wlk. CW4: Holm C 3E 29
    (off London Rd.)
  CW5: Nant 2G 45
    (off Church La.)
  CW8: Crow 3A 6
  CW9: Nort 5A 10
Church Way CW5: Wyb 6H 47
Churchyardside CW5: Nant 2G 45
Churton Cl. CW2: Hou 4C 48
  CW9: Nort 3G 15
Cinder Hill CW8: Whit 3A 18
Cinder La. CW5: Reas 4E 39
  CW9: L Gre .5G 11
Circle, The CW2: Crewe 4B 42
Circle Av. CW5: Will 2E 47
Civic Way CW10: Midd 2A 26
Clare Dr. CW2: Wist 4F 41
Claremont Cl. CW9: Nort 4H 15
Claremont Rd. CW2: Crewe 3H 41
Clarence Gro. CW1: Crewe 6H 35
Clare Pl. CW7: Wins 4D 22
Clary Mdw. CW8: Winn 4G 9
Clatterwick La. CW8: Lit L 4A 2
Claughton Av. CW2: Crewe 3H 41
Clay La. CW1: Hasl 5H 37
  CW8: Whit 4A 18
  CW11: Hasl .1G 37
  CW11: Most .5E 31
Clayton Cl. CW1: Crewe 4G 35
Clayton's Row CW5: Nant 6G 39
    (off Wallfields Rd.)
Cledford Cres. CW10: Midd 5B 26
Cledford La. CW10: Midd 5C 26
Clement Dr. CW1: Crewe 4F 35
Cleveland Way CW7: Wins 4D 22
Cliffe Rd. CW1: Crewe 4H 35
Cliff La. CW8: Act B, Crow 1A 6
Clifford Gro. CW1: Hasl 1G 43
Clifford Pl. CW7: Wins 4E 23
Cliff Rd. CW8: Act B 1B 6
Clifton Av. CW2: Crewe 2H 41
Clifton Dr. CW9: Nort 2A 16
Clifton Rd. CW11: Elw 2H 31
Clifton St. CW2: Crewe 2H 41
Clitheroe Rd. CW8: Weav 4H 7
CLIVE 3D 24
Clive Bk. La. CW7: Wins 4C 24

CLIVE GREEN .4D 24
Clivegreen La. CW7: Wins 3C 24
  CW10: Stan 3C 24
Clive La. CW7: Wins 3C 24
Clonners Fld. CW5: Nant 3H 45
Close, The CW8: Nort 1F 15
Clough Ct. CW5: Nant 2E 45
Clough La. CW8: Nort 1F 15
Clough Rd. CW7: Wins 2G 23
Clough Wlk. CW2: Crewe 5B 42
Cloverdale CW8: Nort 6E 9
Clover Dr. CW7: Wins 6F 19
  WA16: Pick .5F 5
Cloverfields CW1: Hasl 1F 43
Clyde Cres. CW7: Wins 2B 24
Clyde Gro. CW2: Crewe 2G 41
Clydesdale Av. CW2: Crewe 2H 41
Coalpit La. CW10: Stan 4F 25
Coalport Dr. CW7: Wins 6H 19
Cobbles, The CW8: Cudd 3B 12
Cobbs La. CW2: Hou 6C 48
  CW5: Nant 5G 39
Cockington Cl. CW9: Nort 3A 16
Cock La. CW9: Gt B 3H 3
Cockpit La. CW8: Sandi 5F 13
Cocoa Yd. CW5: Nant 2G 45
    (off Hospital St.)
Cogshall La. CW8: And, Comb 6D 2
  CW9: And 6D 2
  CW9: Comb, Lit L 5A 2
Coldmoss Dr. CW11: Sandb 5E 33
COLD MOSS HEATH 4E 33
Coleridge Cl. CW11: Etti H 4G 31
Coleridge Way CW1: Crewe 6D 36
College Flds. CW2: Crewe 4G 41
Colley La. CW11: Blet 4G 33
  CW11: Blet, Sandb 4F 33
Colleys La. CW5: Will 5A 40
Colliers La. CW9: Ast B, Pick 1E 5
Collinbrook Av. CW2: Crewe 4H 41
Collingham Way CW7: Wins 2F 23
Collingtree Av. CW7: Wins 5H 19
Collins St. CW2: Crewe 2G 41
COMBERBACH .4F 3
Comberbach Dr. CW5: Stap 3A 46
Combermere Pl. CW1: Crewe 6A 36
    (off Rigg St.)
Comboy Dr. CW9: Rudh 1C 16
Commons, The CW11: Sandb 3D 32
Commons Mill CW11: Sandb 2D 32
Commonwealth Cl. CW7: Wins 5E 23
Condliffe Cl. CW11: Sandb 4E 33
Congleton Rd. CW11: Arc, Sandb 1G 33
  CW11: Sandb 3D 32
Coningsby Dr. CW7: Wins 3G 23
Coniston Av. CW7: Wins 1E 23
Coniston Cl. CW5: Nant 1A 46
Coniston Dr. CW4: Holm C 3B 28
Conrad Cl. CW1: Crewe 1C 42
Conway Av. CW7: Wins 4E 23
Conway Cl. CW1: Crewe 3A 36
Cooke's La. CW9: L Gre, Rudh 1F 17
Cookesmere La. CW11: Bradw, Sandb 1B 32
Coole La. CW5: Aust 5F 45
Coopers Opening CW11: Sandb 2D 32
    (off Bradwall Rd.)
Cope Av. CW5: Nant 3F 45
Copes La. CW5: Nant 3E 45
Copley Wlk. CW5: Nant 2F 45
    (off Lambert Cres.)
COPPENHALL 5C 36
Coppenhall Gro. CW2: Crewe 1G 41
Coppenhall Heys CW2: Crewe 1G 41
Coppenhall La. CW2: Crewe 1D 40
    (not continuous)
Coppenhall Leisure Cen. 6C 36
COPPENHALL MOSS 2B 36
Copper Wood CW8: Cudd 2C 12
Coppice, The CW5: Nant 4H 45
  CW8: Cudd .2A 12
  CW8: Hart 3B 14
  CW9: Winc 2C 10
  CW11: Sandb 2A 32
Coppice Cl. CW5: Will 1D 46
Coppice Dr. CW10: Midd 5C 26
Coppicemere Dr. CW1: Crewe 3E 43
Coppice Rd. CW5: Will 1D 46

Copyhold CW8: Weav 5H 7
Corfe Way CW7: Wins 4E 23
Coriander Cl. CW10: Midd 1A 26
Cormorant Cl. CW1: Crewe 1D 42
Corners, The CW8: Weav 6A 8
Cornmill Cl. CW11: Warm 2B 30
Cornwall Gro. CW1: Crewe 6H 35
Coronation Av. CW7: Wins 1G 23
Coronation Cres. CW1: Crewe 5C 36
CW11: Sandb 4C 32
Coronation Gro. CW8: Barn 1B 8
Coronation Rd. CW10: Midd 5B 26
Coronation St. CW1: Crewe 6B 36
Coronet Av. CW7: Nort 3H 15
Cotebrook Rd. CW9: Nort 6C 10
Cotswold Cl. CW8: Sandi 5E 13
Cotswold Way CW7: Wins 4D 22
Cottage Cl. CW9: Rudh 5E 11
Cotteril St. CW2: Crewe 3B 42
Cotton La. CW11: Malk B, Sandb 6C 32
Court La. CW8: Weav 4F 7
Courtyard, The CW8: Gors 5E 7
CW10: Bost .4D 20
Coverdale Fold CW11: Etti H 4H 31
Covert Cl. CW7: Wins 3D 22
Cowfields CW5: Nant 1G 45
Cow La. CW7: Wins 3G 23
Cowley Way CW1: Crewe 4C 42
Cowper Cl. CW2: Wist 5G 41
Crabmill Dr. CW11: Elw 2A 32
Crabmill La. CW11: Most 3E 31
Crabmill Rd. CW11: Most, Warm 1C 30
Crabtree Grn. Ct. CW8: Oak 5A 12
Crabtree Grn. Pk. CW8: Oak 6A 12
Crabtree Gro. CW1: Crewe 5C 36
CRANAGE 1C 28
Cranage La. CW9: Nort 4D 10
Cranage Rd. CW2: Crewe 2G 41
Cranborne Rd. CW1: Crewe 5B 36
Cranebrook Cl. CW1: Crewe 3G 35
Cranmere Cl. CW9: Nort 3A 16
Cresanne Cl. CW10: Midd 4B 26
Crescent, The CW5: Nant 1H 45
CW8: Hart 2C 14
CW8: Weav 4H 7
CW9: Nort 1H 15
CW10: Midd .2H 25
Crescent Rd. CW4: Cran 1B 28
Crestwood Cl. CW2: Wist 6H 41
CREWE 1A 42
Crewe Alexandra FC 3B 42
Crewe Bus. Pk. CW1: Crewe 3D 42
Crewe Crematorium & Cemetery
CW1: Crewe .5A 36
Crewe Gates Farm Ind. Est.
CW1: Crewe .3D 42
Crewe Gates Ind. Est.
CW1: Crewe .4E 43
CREWE GREEN 2F 43
Crewe Grn. Av. CW1: Hasl 1F 43
Crewe Grn. Rd. CW1: Crewe 2D 42
Crewe Hall Ent. Pk. CW1: Crewe 1C 42
Crewe Rd. CW1: Crewe 3C 42
CW1: Crewe, Crewe G, Hasl 2E 43
CW2: Shav 4A 48
CW2: Wist 1C 46
CW5: Nant, Will, Wist 2H 45
CW11: Sandb, Whee, Wint 6C 32
Crewe Station (Rail) 3C 42
Crewe St. CW1: Crewe 1B 42
Crewe Swimming Pool 2H 41
Crewe Vagrants Sports Club 4D 46
Crocus St. CW8: Barn 2D 8
Crofters Cl. CW2: Wist 5H 41
WA16: Pick 4G 5
Crofters Ct. CW4: Holm C 2E 29
Crofters Lea CW8: Nort 6F 9
Croftwood Cl. CW7: Wins 3C 22
Cromer Dr. CW1: Crewe 3H 35
Cromwell Cl. CW5: Nant 2G 45
Cromwell Dr. CW2: Shav 3A 48
Cromwell Rd. CW8: Winn 5F 9
Cronkinson Av. CW5: Nant 3H 45
Cronkinson Oak CW5: Nant 3H 45
Crook La. CW7: Wins 1A 24
Crossfield Av. CW7: Wins 4E 23
Crosslands CW1: Hasl 1H 43

Cross La. CW10: Midd 5B 26
CW11: Sandb 4F 33
Cross Rd. CW1: Hasl 1H 43
Cross St. CW1: Hasl 1H 43
CW2: Crewe .2B 42
CW8: Barn 2D 8
CW9: Mars 2C 10
Crossway CW1: Crewe 5B 36
(not continuous)
Cross Wood St. CW5: Nant 2F 45
(off Second Wood St.)
Crotia Av. CW2: West 2F 49
Crowder's La.
CW9: Lach D, Rudh 3F 17
Crowmere Cl. CW8: Sandi 5D 12
Crown Bank CW11: Sandb 3D 32
Crown Dr. CW11: Malk B 6F 33
Crown St. CW9: Nort 4H 9
Crows Nest La. CW9: Comb, Gt B 3F 3
CROWTON 3A 6
Croxton La. CW10: Byl 6G 21
Croxton Way CW8: Hart 3C 14
Crum Hill CW9: Nort 5A 10
Cuckoo La. CW5: Act, Burl 6A 38
CUDDINGTON .3D 12
Cuddington La. CW8: Cudd 4A 12
Cuddington Station (Rail) 3E 13
Culland St. CW2: Crewe 3A 42
Cumberland Av. CW5: Nant 1H 45
Cumberland Cl. CW1: Crewe 6B 36
Cumberland Sports Cen. 6B 36
Cumbermere Dr. CW11: Sandb 2A 32
Curlew Cl. CW7: Wins 6E 23
Curzon Gro. CW7: Wins 2H 23
Cypress M. CW8: Weav 6A 8
(off Northwich Rd.)

D

Dairy Ho. Way CW2: Crewe 3F 41
Dairy La. CW5: Ast M 4A 34
CW5: Ast M, Poole 1D 38
Daisy Bank CW5: Nant 2F 45
Daisybank Dr. CW11: Sandb 3E 33
Daisy Bank La. CW9: And 2E 9
Daisy Cl. WA16: Pick 5F 5
Dalby Ct. CW9: Rudh 2E 17
Dale Ct. CW10: Midd 4B 26
Dalefords La. CW7: Mart 3A 18
CW8: Sandi, Whit 5E 13
CW8: Whit 3A 18
Dale's Sq. CW9: Nort 1H 15
Dale Way CW1: Crewe 6G 35
Dalmahoy Cl. CW7: Wins 1E 23
Dalton Ct. CW11: Sandb 2A 32
Dalton Way CW10: Midd 2B 26
Dane Bank Av. CW2: Crewe 3G 41
Dane Bank Rd. CW9: Nort 6B 10
Dane Cl. CW11: Sandb 2A 32
Danefield Rd. CW4: Holm C 2E 29
CW9: Nort 6B 10
Dane Pl. CW1: Crewe 5B 36
CW7: Wins .2B 24
(off Trent Av.)
Dane St. CW9: Nort 5H 9
CW10: Midd .1B 26
Dappleheath Rd. CW2: Crewe 4G 41
Daresbury Cl. CW4: Holm C 3C 28
Dario Gradi Dr. CW2: Crewe 4B 42
Dark La. CW9: Mars 4C 4
Darley Av. CW2: Crewe 2G 41
Darlington Av. CW1: Crewe 6F 35
Darlington St. CW10: Midd 2A 26
Darnhall School La. CW7: Wins 6E 23
Dart Wlk. CW7: Wins 1A 24
DARWIN St. CW8: Nort 6G 9
DAVENHAM 5H 15
Davenham Ct. CW9: Dave 4A 16
Davenham Cres. CW2: Crewe 2F 41
Davenham Rd. CW9: Nort 4D 16
Davenham Rdbt. CW9: Nort 4H 15
Davenham Way CW10: Midd 6B 26
Davenport Av. CW2: Crewe 5A 42
CW5: Nant 1G 45
Davenport Cl. CW11: Sandb 1F 33
Davenport St. CW1: Crewe 5A 36

David St. CW8: Nort 6G 9
Deadman's La. CW5: Stap 5A 46
Deakins Rd. CW7: Wins 5H 19
(not continuous)
Dean Cl. CW11: Sandb 1A 32
Deane Ct. CW5: Stap 3B 46
Deansgate CW2: Eng B 4H 49
Deans La. CW11: Elw, Sandb 3A 32
Deans Row CW4: Cran 1C 28
Dean St. CW7: Wins 2E 23
CW9: Nort 5C 10
CW10: Midd .1A 26
Dee Cl. CW11: Sandb 1A 32
Dee Sq. CW7: Wins 1A 24
Dee Way CW7: Wins 1A 24
Delaisy Way CW7: Wins 2A 24
Delamere Cl. CW2: Eng B 3H 49
CW8: Barn 2C 8
CW11: Sandb 1B 32
Delamere Ct. CW1: Crewe 1A 42
(off St Mary's St.)
DELAMERE PARK 2B 12
Delamere Pk. Way E. CW8: Cudd 2B 12
Delamere Pk. Way W. CW8: Cudd 3B 12
Delamere Ri. CW7: Wins 2D 22
Delamere Rd. CW5: Nant 3H 45
Delamere St. CW1: Crewe 1A 42
CW7: Wins .2C 22
Dell, The CW8: Cudd 2A 12
Delves Broughton Ct. CW1: Hasl 6H 37
Delves Cl. CW2: Shav 3H 47
Denbigh Cres. CW10: Midd 4A 26
Denbigh Dr. CW7: Wins 4D 22
Dene Dr. CW7: Wins 2F 23
Denehurst Pk. Way CW8: Cudd 2B 12
Denes, The CW7: Wins 3F 23
Denesgate CW7: Wins 3F 23
Deneside Av. CW1: Crewe 5A 36
Denston Cl. CW2: Crewe 4H 41
Denton Cl. CW7: Wins 2E 23
Denton Dr. CW9: Nort 4C 10
Denton Dr. Ind. Est. CW9: Nort 4C 10
Denver Av. CW2: Crewe 2H 41
Derby St. CW1: Crewe 6H 35
Derrington Av. CW2: Crewe 2A 42
Derwent Av. CW7: Wins 2B 24
Derwent Cl. CW4: Holm C 3C 28
CW5: Will 1D 46
Deva Rd. CW2: Crewe 1D 40
Devon Cl. CW10: Midd 1B 26
Dewes St. CW1: Crewe 6H 35
Dexter Way CW10: Midd 1B 26
Dickens Cl. CW11: Etti H 3H 31
Dierdens Ter. CW10: Midd 2A 26
Dierden St. CW7: Wins 2B 24
Dig La. CW5: Act 3A 44
CW5: Burl, Rave 3A 44
CW5: Wyb 4G 47
Dillors Cft. CW1: Leig 2G 35
Dingle, The CW1: Hasl 5H 37
CW8: Barn 1D 8
(off Elmwood Rd.)
Dingle Bank CW11: Sandb 3D 32
(off Dingle La.)
Dingle La. CW7: Wins 2F 23
CW11: Sandb 3E 33
Dingle Wlk. CW7: Wins 2F 23
(in Winsford Cross Shop. Cen.)
Dingle Way CW8: Cudd 2C 12
Diploma Dr. CW10: Midd 1A 26
Dobell's Rd. CW9: Nort 2H 15
(Boardmans Rd.)
CW9: Nort 1H 15
(Lime Av.)
Dock Rd. CW9: Nort 6H 9
Doddington Dr. CW11: Sandb 1E 33
Doddington Rd. CW2: Crewe 2G 41
Dog La. CW4: Holm C 6F 29
CW5: Nant 1G 45
Dorfold Cl. CW11: Sandb 2E 33
Dorfold Dr. CW5: Nant 2F 45
Dorfold Hall 2D 44
Dorfold St. CW1: Crewe 1A 42
Dornoch Ct. CW4: Holm C 4D 28
Dorric Way CW1: Crewe 4A 36
Douglas Cl. CW8: Hart 2E 15
Doulton Cl. CW7: Wins 6H 19

Dove Cl. CW11: Sandb 1C 32
Dovecote Cl. CW2: Wist 5H 41
Dove Pl. CW7: Wins 1B 24
Dover Dr. CW7: Wins 4D 22
Downs, The CW8: Cudd 2B 12
Drake La. CW5: Act 3A 44
Drayton Cres. CW1: Crewe 6D 36
Drillfield Ct. CW9: Nort 5A 10
Drillfield Rd. CW9: Nort 5H 9
Drive, The CW4: Holm C 4E 29
Drovers Way CW11: Sandb 4C 32
Druitt Cl. CW1: Hasl 1H 43
Drumber, The CW7: Wins 2F 23
Drury Cl. CW1: Crewe 1D 42
Drury La. CW1: Crewe 5B 30
Dryden Cl. CW2: Wist 4G 41
Dubthorn La. CW11: Blet 4G 33
Duchy Rd. CW1: Crewe 5E 43
Duddon Cl. CW9: Nort 3G 15
Duke's Cres. CW11: Sandb 1C 32
Duke St. CW2: Crewe 2A 42
Dukes Way CW9: Nort 2G 15
Dunbar Cl. CW4: Holm C 4D 28
Dunham Cl. CW11: Sandb 3E 33
Dunham Ct. CW8: Hart 3B 14
Dunham Cres. CW2: Wist 5H 41
Dunham Rd. CW9: Nort 3H 15
Dunkirk Av. CW7: Wins 3F 23
Dunmore Cl. CW10: Midd 4A 26
Dunnillow Fld. CW5: Nant 3A 46
Dunoon Cl. CW4: Holm C 4D 28
Dunster Cl. CW9: Nort 3A 16
Dunwoody Way CW1: Crewe 6G 35
Durham Dr. CW7: Wins 4E 23
Dutton La. CW8: Crow, Cudd 1A 12
    WA6: Norl 1A 12
Duttons Bus. Cen. CW9: Nort 6H 9
Dutton Way CW1: Crewe 5H 35
    CW5: Nant .4G 45
Dyar Ter. CW8: Winn 4F 9
Dysart Bldgs. CW5: Nant 2G 45

E

Eadie Gro. CW1: Crewe 4G 35
Eaglesfield CW8: Hart 3E 15
Eardley Ct. CW1: Crewe 6H 35
Eardswick La. CW1: Brad G, Mins V 1D 34
Eardswick Rd. CW10: Midd 5A 26
Earles La. CW9: Mars, Winc 5D 4
Earle St. CW1: Crewe 1B 42
Earls Rd. CW2: Shav 3H 47
Earls Way CW9: Nort 3G 15
East Av. CW2: West 2G 49
    CW9: Rudh .1D 16
E. Dudley St. CW7: Wins 2H 23
Eastern Rd. CW2: Shav 2E 47
    CW5: Shav, Will 2E 47
Eastgate Rd. CW4: Holm C 3F 29
East La. CW8: Cudd 4E 13
East Rd. CW10: Midd 2H 25
East Vw. CW5: Nant 1G 45
    (off Scaife Rd.)
Eaton Cl. CW11: Sandb 2E 33
Eaton Ct. CW9: Nort 2G 15
Eaton Cres. CW9: Dave 5G 15
Eaton Dr. CW10: Midd 3H 25
Eaton La. CW9: Dave 5F 15
Eaton Pl. CW8: Hart 3B 14
Eaton St. CW1: Crewe 1A 42
Eaton Vw. CW5: Moul 1G 19
Eccleston Ct. CW9: Nort 2G 15
    (off Harthill Cl.)
Ecton Cl. CW7: Wins 5A 20
Eddisbury Way CW9: Nort 4G 15
Eden Av. CW7: Wins 1H 23
Edenbridge Cl. CW2: West 5F 49
Edenhall Cl. CW4: Holm C 3C 28
Edgewood Dr. CW2: Wist 6G 41
Edinburgh Rd. CW2: Wist 5E 41
Edleston Hall La.
    CW5: Edle, Rave 5B 44
Edleston Rd. CW1: Crewe 2B 42
    CW2: Crewe 2B 42
Edmund Wright Way
    CW5: Nant .2E 45

Edwards Av. CW2: Shav 2A 48
Edwards Cl. CW2: Shav 2A 48
Edward St. CW2: Crewe 3B 42
    CW9: Nort 5C 10
Egerton Av. CW8: Hart 3C 14
Elanor Rd. CW11: Elw 2H 31
Eleanor Cl. CW1: Crewe 6F 35
Electra Ho. CW1: Crewe 3E 43
Electra Way CW1: Crewe 3D 42
Electricity St. CW2: Crewe 2A 42
Elgin Av. CW4: Holm C 4D 28
Eliot Cl. CW1: Crewe 1E 43
Elizabethan Way CW9: Rudh 1E 17
Elizabeth Cl. CW11: Elw 2H 31
Elizabeth St. CW1: Crewe 6H 35
Ellesmere Cl. CW11: Sandb 1A 32
Ellesmere Pl. CW1: Crewe 6A 36
    (off Rigg St.)
Ellesmere Rd. CW9: Nort 3A 16
Ellingham Way CW9: Nort 4G 15
Ellis St. CW1: Crewe 5H 35
Ellwood Grn. CW2: Hou 4C 48
Elm Cl. CW2: Crewe 3E 41
Elm Ct. CW1: Crewe 5B 36
Elm Dr. CW1: Crewe 5B 36
    CW4: Holm C 2F 29
Elm Gro. CW7: Wins 2A 24
Elmore Cl. CW4: Holm C 3D 28
Elmridge Way CW8: Winn 4F 9
Elm Rd. CW8: Weav 6H 7
    CW10: Midd 4B 26
Elmstead Cres. CW1: Crewe 3F 35
Elm St. CW9: Nort 4B 10
Elm Ter. CW1: Crewe 5C 36
Elm Tree La. CW11: Elw 1H 31
Elmwood Gro. CW7: Wins 3H 23
Elmwood Rd. CW8: Barn 1C 8
Elton Crossings Rd. CW11: Elw, Etti H . . .3H 31
Elton Flashes (Nature Reserve) 5F 31
Elton Golf Driving Range 4F 31
Elton Rd. CW11: Etti H 4G 31
Elton La. CW11: Hasl, Wint 1G 37
ELWORTH 2H 31
Elworth Rd. CW11: Elw 3H 31
Elworth St. CW11: Sandb 2C 32
Emerald Dr. CW11: Sandb 1E 33
Emmett St. CW8: Barn 2C 8
Empress Dr. CW2: Crewe 2H 41
Enfield Cl. CW2: Shav 4H 47
Englefield Cl. CW1: Crewe 3G 35
Englesea Gro. CW2: Crewe 4H 41
Ennerdale Cl. CW7: Wins 6F 19
Ennerdale Rd. CW2: Crewe 2E 41
Enterprise Ct. CW11: Elw 2H 31
ERF Way CW10: Midd 3C 26
Eric Dr. CW11: Elw 2H 31
Ernest St. CW2: Crewe 3A 42
Ernley Cl. CW5: Nant 1F 45
Eskdale Cl. CW7: Wins 1E 23
Esk Rd. CW7: Wins 1A 24
Esthers La. CW8: Weav 5H 7
Etherow Cl. CW11: Sandb 2A 32
Eton Ct. CW8: Hart 2E 15
Ettiley Av. CW11: Etti H 4G 31
ETTILEY HEATH 3H 31
Evans St. CW1: Crewe 5H 35
Eva St. CW11: Sandb 1H 31
Everdon Cl. CW7: Wins 5H 19
Evergreens, The CW9: L Gral 2G 11
    (off Langford Av.)
Eyston Cl. CW9: Nort 2G 15

F

Fairacre Dr. CW10: Midd 5C 26
Fairbrook CW2: Crewe 3E 41
Fairburn Av. CW2: Crewe 1F 41
Fairfax Dr. CW5: Nant 1F 45
Fairfield Av. CW11: Sandb 4D 32
Fairfield Rd. CW9: Nort 3A 16
Fairhaven CW2: West 6F 49
Fairholme Rd. CW9: Dave 1A 20
Fairoak Cl. CW7: Wins 3C 22
Fairview Av. CW2: West 2F 49
Fair Vw. Cl. CW8: Barn 2B 8
Fairways, The CW7: Wins 1C 22

Falcon Cl. CW7: Wins 5F 23
    CW10: Midd 6B 26
Falcon Dr. CW1: Crewe 3H 35
Fallon Ct. CW10: Midd 4A 26
Fallowfield Cl. CW7: Wins 2B 22
Fallowfield Ct. CW1: Crewe 5G 35
Falmouth Rd. CW7: Wins 5G 35
Fanshawe Wlk. CW2: Crewe 5A 42
    (off Davenport Av.)
Farley Cl. CW10: Midd 3H 25
Farm Cl. CW8: Weav 4H 7
Farmer Cl. CW2: Crewe 1G 41
Farmleigh Dr. CW1: Crewe 3F 35
Farm Rd. CW8: Weav 4H 7
    CW9: Rudh .6E 11
Farndale Cl. CW2: Wist 1G 47
Farndon Cl. CW8: Cudd 4E 13
Farrier Ct. CW1: Crewe 4B 36
Farriers Way CW7: Wins 2C 22
Farthing La. CW8: Gt B 3B 4
Faulkner Dr. CW10: Midd 5C 26
Fawns Leap CW8: Cudd 2C 12
Felix Rd. CW8: Winn 5G 9
Fernbank Cl. CW1: Crewe 2D 42
    CW7: Wins .2B 24
Fern Ct. CW1: Crewe 2C 42
Ferndale Cl. CW2: West 2F 49
    CW11: Sandb 4E 33
Fernlea Rd. CW9: Mars 5B 4
Fernleigh Cl. CW8: Nort 6E 9
Fernleigh Cl. CW7: Wins 2C 22
    CW10: Midd 5C 26
Fern Way CW8: Weav 4G 7
Fernway CW7: Wins 2B 24
Field Av. CW2: Crewe 4F 41
Field Cl. CW8: Nort 6E 9
Fieldfare CW7: Wins 3A 24
Field La. CW2: Crewe 3D 40
Fields, The CW5: Will 2D 46
Fields Dr. CW11: Sandb 4C 32
Fields Rd. CW1: Hasl 1H 43
Fields Vw. CW5: Wyb 6H 47
    (off Church Way)
Fieldway CW8: Weav 4G 7
Finney's La. CW10: Midd 1H 25
Finsbury Wlk. CW7: Wins 2C 22
Firbeck Gdns. CW2: Crewe 1D 40
Firdale Rd. CW8: Nort 6E 9
Fir Gro. CW8: Weav 5A 8
Fir La. CW8: Sandi 5E 13
First Av. CW1: Crewe 3C 42
    CW11: Sandb 4C 32
First Dig La. CW5: Stap 6C 46
First Wood St. CW5: Nant 2F 45
Firth Cl. CW11: Sandb 2D 32
Firth Flds. CW9: Dave 5H 15
Firthfields Cl. CW9: Dave 5H 15
Fir Tree Cl. CW8: Barn 1D 8
Firtree Cl. CW7: Wins 2B 24
Firwood Wlk. CW2: Crewe 5A 42
Fitness First
    Crewe 1E 41
Fitton St. CW9: L Gral 3G 11
Flag La. CW1: Crewe 1A 42
    CW2: Crewe 2A 42
Flat La. CW11: Sandb 3D 32
    (not continuous)
Flavian Cl. CW10: Midd 1A 26
Flea La. CW10: Midd 3A 26
    (off Long La.)
Fletcher Gro. CW9: Rudh 1C 16
Fletcher St. CW1: Crewe 6H 35
Flixton Dr. CW2: Crewe 3G 41
Flour Mill Way CW1: Crewe 2E 43
Flowerscroft CW5: Nant 3A 46
Flowers La. CW1: Brad G, Leig 1E 35
Flower St. CW8: Nort 6F 9
Fodens Ter. CW11: Sandb 2C 32
Ford Cl. CW1: Crewe 6H 35
Ford Ct. CW7: Wins 5E 23
Ford La. CW1: Crewe 6H 35
Forest Cl. CW8: Cudd 4D 12
Forest Hill CW8: Hart 4H 13
Forest Pl. CW9: Nort 4A 10
Forest Rd. CW7: Wins 3D 22
    CW8: Cudd, Oak 5C 12
Forest Rd. Pk. CW8: Oak 5C 12

Forest St. CW8: Weav 5G 7
Forest Vw. Cvn. Site CW8: Cudd 4A 12
Forge Flds. CW11: Sandb 6B 32
Forge St. CW1: Crewe 1B 42
Forster Av. CW8: Weav 5A 8
Fossa Cl. CW10: Midd 1A 26
Foulkes Av. CW1: Crewe 5F 35
Foundry La. CW11: Elw 2H 31
Fountain Ct. CW7: Wins 2F 23
                    (off Dene Dr.)
  CW9: Dave 5H 15
Fountain La. CW9: Dave 5H 15
Fountains Cl. CW10: Midd 2G 25
Fourseasons Cl. CW2: Wist 5H 41
Fourth Av. CW1: Crewe 4D 42
Fourways CW2: West 2F 49
Fowler Cl. CW2: Crewe 4B 42
Fox Covert Way CW1: Leig 2G 35
Foxendale Cl. CW8: Nort 6F 9
Foxes Fold CW8: Winn 4G 9
Foxes Hey CW8: Cudd 2B 12
Foxes Hollow CW1: Crewe 4C 36
Foxfield La. CW7: Wins 2B 22
Foxglove Cl. CW2: Wist 6H 41
Foxhill Cl. CW8: Sandi 5E 13
Foxlea CW3: Comb 4E 3
FOXWIST GREEN 3A 18
Foxwist Grn. CW8: Whit 3A 18
Frances St. CW2: Crewe 3B 42
Frank Bott Av. CW1: Crewe 4G 35
Franklin M. CW9: Nort 4C 10
Franklyn Av. CW2: Crewe 2H 41
Frank Webb Av. CW1: Crewe 5G 35
Freshfields CW2: Wist 6G 41
  CW9: Comb 4E 3
Freshwater Dr. CW2: West 6F 49
Freshwater Vw. CW8: Nort 5H 9
Friars Cl. CW2: Wist 5F 41
Frida Cres. CW8: Nort 1G 15
Frog La. WA16: Pick 3F 5
Front St. CW11: Sandb 3E 33
Fryer Rd. CW9: L Gral 2G 11
Fulbeck Cl. CW2: Wist 5H 41
Fuller Dr. CW2: Wist 5G 41
Fullerton Rd. CW8: Hart 2B 14
Fulton Gro. CW9: Dave 5H 15
Funsters 2A 42
Furber St. CW1: Crewe 6A 36
Furness Cl. CW4: Holm C 3C 28
  CW7: Wins 3D 22
Furnival St. CW2: Crewe 3A 42
  CW11: Sandb 2D 32

G

Gable Ct. CW5: Nant 1G 45
          (off Lady Helen Wlk.)
Gadbrook Bus. Cen. CW9: Rudh 2D 16
Gadbrook Pk. CW9: Rudh 2D 16
Gadbrook Rd. CW9: Rudh 1D 16
Gainsborough Rd. CW2: Crewe 2G 41
Galloway Cl. CW4: Holm C 4E 29
  CW10: Midd 1C 26
Gallowsclough La. CW8: Oak 4A 12
Galway Gro. CW2: Shav 3H 47
Game St. CW11: Sandb 6C 32
Gardens, The CW11: Sandb 3D 32
Garfit St. CW10: Midd 1B 26
Garnett Cl. CW5: Stap 3H 45
Gatefield St. CW1: Crewe 1A 42
Gateway CW1: Crewe 3D 42
Gawsworth Av. CW2: Crewe 2F 41
Gawsworth Cl. CW4: Holm C 3D 28
  CW9: Nort 3A 16
Gawsworth Dr. CW11: Sandb 2E 33
Geneva Rd. CW7: Wins 3E 23
George VI Av. CW10: Midd 5B 26
George VI Cl. CW10: Midd 5B 26
George's La. CW9: Ast B 2D 4
George St. CW7: Wins 2G 23
  CW8: Barn 2D 8
  CW11: Elw 1A 32
George's Wlk. CW11: Sandb 3D 32
               (off High St.)
Gerard Dr. CW5: Nant 3E 45

Gerrard Dr. CW8: Weav 4H 7
Gibb Hill CW9: Antr, Comb 3F 3
Gibbon Dr. CW9: L Gral 2G 11
Gibson Cl. CW5: Nant 1F 45
Gibson Cres. CW11: Elw 3H 31
Gillow Cl. CW1: Crewe 3G 35
Gingerbread La. CW5: Nant 2A 46
Gladstone St. CW1: Crewe 1A 42
  CW5: Will 1D 46
  CW7: Wins 4F 23
  CW8: Nort 6F 9
Glaisdale Cl. CW2: Wist 1G 47
Glamis Cl. CW2: Wist 5E 41
Glastonbury Dr. CW10: Midd 2H 25
Gleave Rd. CW8: Weav 4H 7
Glebe Cl. CW5: Wyb 6G 47
          (off Church Way)
Glebe Grn. Dr. CW7: Wins 5E 23
Glebe Rd. CW8: Cudd 3E 13
Glencoe Cl. CW4: Holm C 4D 28
Glendale Cl. CW2: Crewe 2D 40
Gleneagles Dr. CW4: Holm C 4D 28
  CW7: Wins 1E 23
Glenorchy Cl. CW4: Holm C 4E 29
Glover St. CW1: Crewe 6G 35
Goddard Ct. CW1: Crewe 6H 35
Goddard St. CW1: Crewe 6H 35
Godwin Cres. CW2: Shav 3A 48
Goldcrest Cl. CW7: Wins 6E 23
Golden Hill CW2: Eng B 4H 49
Goldsmith Dr. CW11: Elw 3H 31
Goode Way CW2: Crewe 4B 42
Goodwood Cl. CW8: Barn 2D 8
Goodwood Ri. CW10: Midd 1G 25
Goosebrook Cl. CW9: Comb 3E 3
Goosebrook La. CW9: Antr 1A 2
  WA4: High W 1A 2
Gordale Cl. CW8: Winn 5F 9
Gorse Covert CW9: Winc 2C 10
Gorsey Bank Cres. CW5: Wyb 6G 47
Gorsley Cl. CW10: Midd 5A 26
GORSTAGE 1G 13
Gorstage La. CW8: Gors 5G 7
Goulden St. CW1: Crewe 6G 35
Gowy Cl. CW11: Sandb 1A 32
Gowy Wlk. CW7: Wins 6A 20
Grace Cl. CW1: Hasl 1G 43
Grainger's Rd. CW9: Nort 2H 15
Grampian Way CW7: Wins 4C 22
Grand Junc. Retail Pk. CW1: Crewe 1B 42
Grand Junc. Way CW1: Crewe 1C 42
Grange, The CW8: Hart 2D 14
Grange Av. CW8: Barn 2C 8
Grangebrook Dr. CW7: Wins 6E 19
Grange Cl. CW1: Crewe 2C 42
  CW2: Eng B 3H 49
  CW11: Sandb 2B 32
Grange Ct. CW7: Wins 2D 22
Grange Dr. CW8: Hart 1C 14
Grange La. CW7: Wins 6E 19
  CW8: Gors 6E 7
          (not continuous)
  CW8: Whit 2B 18
Grange Lea CW10: Midd 2H 25
Grange Rd. CW8: Barn 2C 8
  CW8: Cudd 5D 12
  CW9: Rudh 1D 16
Grange Way CW11: Sandb 2B 32
Grantham Cl. CW9: Nort 6C 10
Granville Rd. CW9: Nort 2A 16
Granville Sq. CW7: Wins 3F 23
Granville St. CW7: Wins 3G 23
Grasmere Av. CW2: Crewe 6F 35
Grasmere Cl. CW7: Wins 1F 23
Grasmere Dr. CW4: Holm C 3C 28
GRAVEL 2A 24
GREAT BUDWORTH 3B 4
GREEN, THE 5F 39
Green, The CW8: Hart 2D 14
  CW10: Midd 5B 26
Greenacres CW1: Crewe 5A 36
  CW11: Sandb 2C 32
Greenall Rd. CW9: Nort 5B 10
Green Av. CW8: Barn 2C 8
  CW9: Dave 4G 15
Greenbank Cl. CW5: Will 1D 46
Greenbank La. CW8: Nort 1E 15

Greenbank Pk. CW11: Whee 6C 32
Greenbank Station (Rail) 1F 15
Greendale Dr. CW10: Midd 4H 25
Greendale Gdns. CW1: Crewe 5C 36
Greenfields CW7: Wins 2B 24
Greenfields Av. CW2: Shav 3H 47
Greenfield Way CW8: Cudd 3E 13
Green La. CW5: Edle 3D 44
  CW5: Will 2D 46
  CW9: Dave 4H 15
  CW9: Winc 1E 11
  CW11: Most, Warm 2D 30
Greenlaw Cl. CW9: Nort 2A 16
Green Pk. CW8: Weav 6A 8
Greenside Dr. CW9: L Gre 5G 11
Green St. CW11: Sandb 2D 32
Green Wlk. CW8: Cudd 3F 13
Greenway CW1: Crewe 5B 36
Greenway Dr. CW9: Nort 6C 10
Greenway Wlk. CW9: Nort 6C 10
Greenwood Cl. CW8: Weav 4H 7
Grenville Cl. CW1: Hasl 6G 37
Gresty Bldgs. CW5: Nant 1G 45
           (off Cowfields)
Gresty Grn. Rd. CW2: Shav 5B 42
Gresty La. CW2: Shav 1G 47
Gresty Rd. CW2: Crewe 3B 42
Gresty Side CW5: Nant 2E 45
Gresty Ter. CW1: Crewe 2C 42
Greville Dr. CW7: Wins 2A 24
Greystone Pk. CW1: Crewe 1B 42
Griffiths Dr. CW9: Rudh 1D 16
Griffiths Rd. CW9: L Gral, L Gre, Rudh . . .6E 11
Grizedale Cl. CW2: Crewe 3D 40
Groby Rd. CW1: Crewe 1B 36
Grocott's Row CW5: Nant 2G 45
Grosvenor Av. CW8: Hart 3C 14
Grosvenor Ct. CW1: Crewe 6H 35
  CW7: Wins 4E 23
Grosvenor St. CW1: Crewe 6H 35
  CW7: Wins 3G 23
Grove, The CW9: Dave 5A 16
Grove Av. CW9: L Gral 2G 11
Grove Cl. CW7: Wins 3D 22
Grovemount CW9: Dave 5H 15
Guernsey Cl. CW10: Midd 1B 26
Guillemot Cl. CW1: Crewe 6D 36
Gullet, The CW5: Nant 2G 45
Gutterscroft CW1: Hasl 6H 37

H

Haddon Cl. CW2: Wist 6H 41
  CW4: Holm C 3D 28
Hadfield St. CW9: Nort 4B 10
Hadley Dr. CW2: Eng B 3H 49
Hadrian Way CW8: Sandi 5F 13
  CW10: Midd 1A 26
Haighton Cl. CW5: Nant 1G 45
Hallams Dr. CW5: Stap 3B 46
Hall Dr. CW5: Will 1C 46
  CW9: Mars 5B 4
Hall La. CW1: Warm 6C 30
  CW7: Darn 6E 23
  CW9: Antr, Lit L 4B 2
  CW9: L Gral, Winc 1E 11
  CW11: Most, Sandb 4E 31
  WA16: Pick 2H 5
Hall O'Shaw St. CW1: Crewe 1C 42
Hallshaw Av. CW1: Crewe 6C 36
Halls Pl. CW9: Nort 6H 9
Hall Vw. Cl. CW8: Gors 6E 7
Halton Dr. CW2: Crewe 6D 34
Hambleton Way CW7: Wins 4C 22
Hamilton Cl. CW1: Hasl 1G 43
Hammond St. CW2: Crewe 2A 42
Hampstead Ct. CW7: Wins 3C 22
Hanbury Cl. CW2: Wist 6H 41
Handforth Rd. CW2: Crewe 2E 41
Handley Hill CW7: Wins 3D 22
Hangman's La. CW9: L Gre 6H 11
Hankelow Cl. CW10: Midd 5A 26
Hannah's Wlk. CW10: Midd 3H 25
          (off St Ann's Rd.)
Hanover Dr. CW7: Wins 5F 23
Harding Rd. CW5: Nant 3E 45

Hardwicke Ct.—Hurdsfield Cl.

Hardwicke Ct. CW1: Crewe 1C 42
Hardy Cl. CW2: Wist 5F 41
Hareswood Cl. CW7: Wins 2C 22
Harewood Cl. CW9: Nort 2H 15
Hargrave Av. CW2: Crewe 2F 41
Hargreaves Rd. CW9: Nort 5C 10
Harlequin Theatre
Northwich 6H 9
Harris Cl. CW1: Leig 2H 35
Harrison Dr. CW1: Crewe 1H 41
Harrisons Pl. CW8: Nort 5G 9
Harris Rd. CW9: L Gral 3G 11
Harrow Cl. CW2: Crewe 4G 41
Harrow Way CW9: Nort 4G 15
HARTFORD 3C 14
HARTFORDBEACH 1C 14
Hartford Bus. Cen. CW8: Hart 3B 14
Hartford Cl. CW11: Sandb 2E 33
Hartford Rd. CW9: Dave 4F 15
Hartford Station (Rail) 3C 14
Harthill Cl. CW9: Nort 2G 15
Hartwell Gro. CW7: Wins 5H 19
Harvest Cl. CW9: Moul 1H 19
Harvey Av. CW5: Nant 1A 46
Haslemere Way CW1: Crewe 5B 36
HASLINGTON 1H 43
Hassall Rd. CW11: Malk B, Sandb 6E 33
Hastings Rd. CW5: Nant 2H 45
Hatchmere Cl. CW11: Sandb 2B 32
Hatfield Ct. CW4: Holm C 3C 28
Hatherton Cl. CW9: Nort 3H 15
Hatton La. CW8: Nort 1F 15
Haven, The CW1: Crewe 4B 36
Haverhill Cl. CW2: West 4F 49
Haweswater Av. CW1: Leig 2H 35
Haweswater Dr. CW7: Wins 1F 23
Hawksey Dr. CW5: Nant, Stap 3H 45
Hawkshead Way CW7: Wins 1F 23
Hawk St. CW11: Sandb 3D 32
Hawthorn Av. *CW5: Nant* *2H 45*
(off Crewe Rd.)
Hawthorn Cl. CW4: Holm C 3F 29
CW7: Wins 6E 19
Hawthorne Dr. CW11: Sandb 3E 33
Hawthorne Gro. CW7: Wins 2A 24
CW8: Barn 1B 8
Hawthorn Gro. CW1: Crewe 4B 36
Hawthorn La. CW2: Crewe 3F 41
Hawthorn Rd. CW8: Weav 5G 7
Hawthorns, The CW1: Hasl 6H 37
CW8: Nort 6E 9
Hawthorn Vs. CW4: Holm C 3E 29
Hawthorn Wlk. CW9: Winc 2C 10
Haydn Jones Dr. CW5: Nant 3H 45
Hayes Cl. CW5: Nant 6G 39
Hayes Dr. CW8: Barn 2D 8
Hayhurst Av. CW10: Midd 3H 25
Hayhurst Cl. CW9: Nort 5H 9
Hayling Cl. CW1: Crewe 3H 35
HAYMOOR GREEN 5E 47
Haymoor Grn. Rd. CW5: Wyb 5E 47
Hazel Dr. CW7: Wins 3E 23
CW8: Weav 6H 7
Hazel Gro. CW1: Crewe 4A 36
Hazelmere Cl. CW8: Hart 2E 15
Hazelwood Rd. CW8: Barn 1D 8
Headworth Cl. CW9: Nort 3H 15
Healey Cl. CW1: Crewe 3G 35
Heath Av. CW11: Sandb 3G 33
Heathbank Cotts. *CW5: Nant* *1H 45*
(off Birchin La.)
Heathbrook CW9: Rudh 6D 10
Heath Cl. CW11: Sandb 3F 33
Heathcote Gdns. CW9: Rudh 6D 10
Heathergate Pl. CW2: Wist 5H 41
Heathfield Av. CW1: Crewe 1H 41
Heathfield Cl. CW5: Nant 1H 45
Heath La. CW9: Budw H, Gt B 2A 4
Heath Rd. CW8: Weav 4A 8
CW11: Sandb 3F 33
Heathside CW5: Nant 1H 45
Heath St. CW1: Crewe 1B 42
Heath Vw. CW1: Hasl 2H 43
Heaton Cl. CW10: Midd 5A 26
Heaton Sq. CW7: Wins 3F 23
Heaton Way CW2: Eng B 3H 49
Heaward Cl. CW2: Shav 3H 47
HEBDEN GREEN 4B 22
Heber Wlk. CW9: Nort 5A 10
Hedgerow Dr. CW9: Winc 2C 10
Hefferston Grange Dr. CW8: Gors 6E 7
Hefferston Ri. CW8: Gors 6E 7
Hellath Wen CW5: Nant 5G 45
Helmdon Cl. CW7: Wins 6H 19
Helmsdale Cl. CW1: Crewe 5H 35
Helton Cl. CW4: Holm C 3C 28
Hemming St. CW8: Winn 4F 9
Hemswell Cl. CW7: Wins 3G 23
Henbury Cl. CW10: Midd 4A 26
Hendon Cl. CW1: Crewe 6D 36
Henley Dr. CW7: Wins 2H 23
Henley Rd. CW2: West 6F 49
Henry St. CW1: Crewe 6B 36
CW1: Hasl 1H 43
Henshall Dr. CW11: Sandb 1E 33
Henshalls Way CW5: Nant 3F 45
Herald Dr. CW1: Crewe 2C 42
Herbert St. CW1: Crewe 6D 36
CW9: L Gral 3G 11
Herbert Swindells Cl. CW2: Crewe 4B 42
Herdman St. CW2: Crewe 3B 42
Hereford Way CW10: Midd 1C 26
Hermitage Ct. CW4: Holm C 3F 29
Hermitage Dr. CW4: Holm C 2F 29
Hermitage La. CW4: Holm C 1F 29
Heron Cl. CW7: Wins 6F 23
Heron Cres. CW1: Crewe 6D 36
Herrick Cl. CW2: Wist 5G 41
Hesketh Cft. CW1: Crewe 3G 35
Hesketh Dr. CW9: L Gral 2G 11
Hewitt Dr. CW7: Wins 3D 24
Hewitt Gro. CW9: Winc 6F 5
Hewitt St. CW2: Crewe 3B 42
CW9: Nort 3D 10
Heyes Pk. CW8: Hart 3B 14
Heyeswood La. CW8: Hart 3C 14
Heysoms Av. CW8: Nort 1F 15
Heysoms Cl. CW8: Nort 1F 15
Heywood Grn. *CW2: Crewe* *5A 42*
(off Brookhouse Dr.)
Hickson St. CW8: Barn 2D 8
Hidcote Cl. CW2: Wist 5H 41
Hield Gro. CW9: Ast B 3C 4
Hield La. CW9: Ast B 4C 4
Highbank Cl. CW8: Barn 2D 8
Highbank Rd. CW8: Nort 6F 9
HIGHER MARSTON 5B 4
HIGHER SHURLACH 2D 16
HIGHER WINCHAM 6F 5
Highfield Av. CW9: L Gral 2G 11
Highfield Dr. CW5: Nant 1H 45
Highfield Pl. CW8: Nort 6G 9
Highfield Rd. CW8: Nort 6H 9
Highgate Cl. CW1: Crewe 3G 35
High St. CW2: Crewe 2B 42
CW5: Nant 2G 45
(not continuous)
CW7: Wins 2E 23
CW8: Weav 4G 7
CW9: Gt B 4A 4
CW9: Nort 5H 9
CW11: Sandb 3D 32
Hightown CW1: Crewe 1A 42
CW10: Midd 2A 26
CW11: Sandb 3D 32
Hill, The CW11: Blet, Sandb 3E 33
Hillcrest Av. CW4: Holm C 3D 28
Hillfield Gdns. CW5: Nant 3G 45
Hillfield Pl. CW5: Nant 3G 45
Hillfield Vw. CW5: Nant 3G 45
Hillside CW8: Nort 6E 9
Hillside Dr. CW1: Crewe 6C 36
Hillside La. CW9: Moul 2G 19
Hill St. CW1: Crewe 1B 42
CW7: Wins 2H 23
CW11: Elw 2H 31
Hill Top CW8: Barn 2D 8
Hill Top Av. CW7: Wins 2E 23
Hilltop Pk. WA16: Pick 4F 5
Hill Top Rd. CW8: Act B 2D 6
Hill Vw. Ri. CW8: Winn 4G 9
Hilton Cl. CW10: Midd 3H 25
Hinchley Cl. CW8: Hart 2C 14
Hinde St. CW5: Nant 3F 45
Hind Heath La. CW11: Sandb 5B 32
Hind Heath Rd. CW11: Sandb 4A 32
Hindley Cres. CW8: Barn 2C 8
Hinton Rd. CW2: Crewe 5B 42
Hirsch Cl. CW5: Nant 2A 46
Hobbs Cl. CW1: Hasl 1G 43
Hodge La. CW8: Gors, Hart 1G 13
Hodgkin Cl. CW5: Nant 3H 45
Hogshead La. CW8: Oak 6A 12
Holbury Cl. CW1: Crewe 3H 35
Holcot Ct. CW7: Wins 5A 20
Hole Ho. La. CW8: Lit L 1A 8
Holford Av. CW9: L Gral 2G 11
Holkam Cl. CW9: Nort 2H 15
Holland Cl. CW11: Sandb 4E 33
Hollands Rd. CW9: Nort 6H 9
Holland St. CW1: Crewe 5H 35
Holland Wlk. CW5: Nant 1F 45
Hollies, The CW2: Shav 3H 47
CW9: Moul 1G 19
CW9: Nort 1G 15
Hollow Oak La. CW8: Cudd 3B 12
Hollybank Cl. CW8: Winn 4F 9
Hollybush Cres. CW5: Will 2D 46
Holly Ct. CW8: Sandi 5E 13
CW10: Midd 1H 25
Holly Dr. CW7: Wins 3F 23
Holly Heath Cl. CW11: Sandb 4E 33
Holly Mt. CW2: Shav 2C 48
Holly Rd. CW8: Weav 5G 7
Holly Wlk. CW8: Nort 6E 9
HOLMES CHAPEL 3E 29
Holmes Chapel Bus. Pk. CW4: Holm C 3F 29
Holmes Chapel Leisure Cen. 4C 28
Holmes Chapel Rd. CW4: Holm C 5H 29
CW4: Spro 2B 26
CW10: Midd 2B 26
CW11: Sandb 1G 33
Holmes Chapel Station (Rail) 3F 29
Holmlea Dr. CW1: Crewe 2D 42
Holt St. CW1: Crewe 1H 41
Holyrood Dr. CW2: Wist 5E 41
Home Farm La. CW8: Cudd 2A 12
Homestead Ct. *CW9: Nort* *6D 10*
(off Middlewich Rd.)
Homewood Cres. CW8: Hart 2D 14
Honiton Way CW10: Midd 1B 26
Hooker St. CW8: Nort 6G 9
Hope St. CW2: Crewe 3B 42
CW8: Nort 6G 9
CW11: Sandb 3D 32
Hopley Ct. *CW2: Crewe* *3A 42*
(off Stalbridge Rd.)
Hornbeam Dr. CW8: Hart 3A 14
Hornby Dr. CW5: Nant 2A 46
Horton Way CW5: Stap 3A 46
Hospital La. CW5: Rave 5A 44
Hospital St. CW1: Crewe 5B 36
CW5: Nant 2G 45
Hothersall Cl. CW1: Leig 2H 35
HOUGH 5C 48
Hough La. CW8: And, Barn 6D 2
CW9: And, Barn, Comb 5B 2
Houghton Cl. CW9: Nort 3H 15
Houndings La. CW11: Sandb 5C 32
Hove Cl. CW1: Crewe 3H 35
Howard St. CW1: Crewe 6D 36
Howbeck Cres. CW5: Wyb 6G 47
Howbeck Wlk. *CW2: Crewe* *5B 42*
(off Davenport Av.)
Hubert Dr. CW10: Midd 3A 26
Hughes Dr. CW2: Crewe 1F 41
Hulme St. CW1: Crewe 6F 35
Hungerford Av. CW1: Crewe 1C 42
Hungerford Pl. CW11: Sandb 4C 32
Hungerford Rd. CW1: Crewe 1C 42
Hungerford Ter. CW1: Crewe 1D 42
Hunter Av. CW2: Shav 6B 42
Huntersfield CW2: Shav 4H 47
CW8: Nort 6F 9
Hunters Hill CW8: Weav 4G 7
Hunters Ri. CW7: Wins 2E 23
Hunting Lodge M. CW8: Cudd 3E 13
Huntsbank Bus. Pk. CW2: Wist 6E 41
Hunt's La. CW8: Gors 4F 13
Hunts Lock CW9: Nort 1H 15
Hurdsfield Cl. CW10: Midd 4A 26

58 A-Z Crewe

Hurleston Bldgs. *CW5: Nant* 1G **45**
(off Weaver Rd.)
Hurn Cl. *CW1: Crewe* 3H **35**
Hutchins' Cl. *CW10: Midd* 5C **26**
Huxley St. *CW8: Nort* 6G **9**
Hythe Av. *CW1: Crewe* 3H **35**

I

Imperial Ct. *CW5: Nant* 2H **45**
Imperial M. *CW2: Crewe* 2B **42**
(off Lord St.)
Ingleton Cl. *CW4: Holm C* 3C **28**
Inglewood Av. *CW10: Midd* 6B **26**
Ion Path *CW7: Wins* 2C **24**
Ironbridge Dr. *CW4: Holm C* 4E **29**
Ivatt Ho. *CW1: Crewe* 1H **41**
(off Blount Cl.)
Ivy Dr. *CW8: Sandi* 5E **13**

J

Jack La. *CW2: West* 1G **49**
CW9: Bost, Dave, Moul 1A **20**
CW10: Bost 4B **20**
Jackson Av. *CW5: Nant* 2H **45**
Jacobs Way *WA16: Pick* 4F **5**
James Atkinson Way *CW1: Crewe* . . .4F **35**
James Hall St. *CW5: Nant* 1G **45**
James St. *CW9: Nort* 5C **10**
Jan Palach Av. *CW5: Nant* 3H **45**
Jersey Way *CW10: Midd* 1B **26**
Jesmond Cres. *CW2: Crewe* 3H **41**
Jessop Way *CW1: Hasl* 1G **43**
Jodrell Cl. *CW4: Holm C* 3C **28**
John Brunner Cres. *CW8: Nort* 1G **15**
John Fryer Av. *CW9: Winc* 6G **5**
John Gresty Dr. *CW5: Will* 1D **46**
John St. *CW1: Crewe* 4A **36**
(Meredith St.)
CW1: Crewe 1A **42**
(Victoria St.)
CW7: Wins 2E **23**
CW9: Nort 5H **9**
(off Crum Hill)
Jones's La. *CW4: Midd* 4H **27**
CW10: Midd 4H **27**
Joyce Av. *CW7: Wins* 1E **23**
Jubilee Av. *CW2: Crewe* 2H **41**
Jubilee Ct. *CW4: Holm C* 3C **28**
Jubilee Gdns. *CW5: Nant* 3G **45**
Jubilee Ter. *CW5: Nant* 3G **45**
Jubilee Way *CW7: Wins* 2F **23**
(off The Drumber)

K

Keats Dr. *CW2: Wist* 5G **41**
Keats La. *CW9: Winc* 6G **5**
Keeper's La. *CW8: Weav* 5A **8**
Keepers Wlk. *CW8: Weav* 6B **8**
Kelsborrow Cl. *CW9: Nort* 4G **15**
Kelstern Cl. *CW9: Nort* 5B **10**
Kemble Cl. *CW2: Wist* 5H **41**
Kempton Av. *CW1: Crewe* 4A **36**
Kendal Way *CW2: West* 6G **49**
Kendrick Cl. *CW8: Weav* 4H **7**
Kenilworth Cl. *CW2: Wist* 6G **41**
Kenmare Bank *CW9: Nort* 2A **16**
Kennel La. *CW8: Sandi* 6E **13**
Kennelwood Rd. *CW9: Comb* 4E **3**
Kensington Cl. *CW5: Nant* 1G **45**
(off Dog La.)
CW7: Wins 4E **23**
Kensington Dr. *CW5: Will* 3D **46**
Kensington Way *CW9: Nort* 4G **15**
Kentmere Av. *CW7: Wins* 1F **23**
Kents Ash *CW7: Wins* 4E **23**
Kent's La. *CW1: Crewe* 2A **36**
Kerridge Cl. *CW10: Midd* 3H **25**
Kestrel Cl. *CW7: Wins* 6E **23**
CW10: Midd 5B **26**
Kestrel Dr. *CW1: Crewe* 3H **35**
Kestrel Rd. *CW8: Nort* 6E **9**

Keswick Cl. *CW2: Crewe* 2E **41**
CW7: Wins 1E **23**
Kettell Av. *CW1: Crewe* 5F **35**
Kidston Dr. *CW1: Crewe* 4F **35**
Kiln La. *CW5: Wyb* 6H **47**
Kinder Dr. *CW2: Crewe* 2D **40**
Kinderton Mobile Home Pk. *CW10: Midd* .4E **27**
Kinderton St. *CW10: Midd* 2A **26**
King Edward Cl. *CW9: Nort* 2H **15**
King Edward St. *CW10: Midd* 2A **26**
Kingfisher Cl. *CW5: Nant* 5G **39**
Kingfisher Ct. *CW9: Nort* 3C **10**
Kingfisher Dr. *CW7: Wins* 5F **23**
Kingfisher Gro. *CW9: Winc* 6F **5**
King George Av. *CW9: Nort* 5B **10**
King Pl. *CW5: Nant* 1G **45**
Kings Ct. *CW5: Nant* 2F **45**
King's Cres. *CW10: Midd* 1A **26**
Kingsdown Cl. *CW2: West* 6G **49**
Kings Dr. *CW2: Wist* 5E **41**
King's Ga. *CW8: Sandi* 5E **13**
King's La. *CW5: Nant* 2F **45**
Kingslawn Cl. *CW9: Nort* 2H **15**
Kingsley Cl. *CW8: Hart* 2E **15**
Kingsley Ct. *CW11: Elw* 1H **31**
Kingsley Rd. *CW1: Hasl* 1G **43**
CW8: Crow 3A **6**
KINGSLEY VILLAGE 1F **45**
Kingsley Wlk. *CW7: Wins* 1D **22**
(not continuous)
KINGSMEAD 3G **15**
Kingsmead *CW9: Nort* 2H **15**
Kingsmead Crossroads *CW9: Dave* . . .3H **15**
Kings Mdw. *CW7: Hou* 5C **48**
Kingsmead Sq. *CW9: Nort* 3G **15**
King St. *CW8: Hart* 2D **14**
CW9: Rudh, What, Lach D 6E **11**
CW10: Byl 3H **21**
CW10: Midd 1A **26**
CW11: Elw 1A **32**
King St. Trad. Est. *CW10: Midd* 1B **26**
Kingsway *CW2: Crewe* 2H **41**
CW7: Wins 2H **23**
CW9: Nort 5B **10**
Kingswood Av. *CW2: West* 4F **49**
Kingswood Cres. *CW10: Midd* 6C **26**
Kinloch Cl. *CW1: Crewe* 5H **35**
Kintore Cl. *CW7: Wins* 1A **24**
Kipling Way *CW1: Crewe* 1D **42**
Kitfield Av. *CW10: Midd* 4A **26**
Knightsbridge Av. *CW9: Nort* 4G **15**
Knights Grange Sports Complex 6D **18**
Knights Mdw. *CW7: Wins* 6E **19**
Knights Way *CW2: Shav* 4H **47**
Knutsford Rd. *CW4: Cran, Holm C* 1C **28**
CW9: Antr, Ast B, Budw H 1G **3**

L

Laburnum Av. *CW2: Crewe* 3F **41**
CW5: Nant 2H **45**
(off Crewe Rd.)
Laburnum Cres. *CW8: Barn* 2D **8**
Laburnum Gro. *CW1: Crewe* 5B **36**
CW8: Weav 5H **7**
Laburnum Rd. *CW9: Dave* 4H **15**
CW9: Rudh 1C **16**
Ladies Wlk. *CW10: Midd* 4H **25**
Lady Helen Wlk. *CW5: Nant* 1G **45**
Lagos Gro. *CW7: Wins* 1G **23**
Laidon Av. *CW2: Wist* 5G **41**
Lake Ho. Cl. *CW8: Weav* 4H **7**
Lakemoor Country Pk. 2H **37**
Lakeside Cvn. Pk. *CW7: Wins* 4H **23**
Lakeside Vw. *CW5: Nant* 4G **45**
CW9: Moul 2H **19**
Lambert Cres. *CW5: Nant* 1E **45**
Lambert Way *CW8: Hart* 3C **14**
Lambourn Dr. *CW1: Leig* 2H **35**
Lambourne Gro. *CW10: Midd* 2H **25**
Lancaster Cl. *CW7: Wins* 5F **23**
Lancaster Flds. *CW1: Crewe* 3D **42**
Landswood Pk. *CW8: Hart* 3D **14**
LANE ENDS 6B **30**
Langdale Cl. *CW7: Wins* 1F **23**

Langdale Rd. *CW2: Crewe* 3D **40**
Langford Rd. *CW9: L Gral* 2G **11**
Langley Cl. *CW11: Sandb* 1E **33**
Langley Dr. *CW2: Crewe* 3G **41**
Langley Rd. *CW9: Nort* 1A **16**
Lansdowne Rd. *CW1: Crewe* 6D **36**
Lapwing Cl. *CW7: Wins* 6E **23**
Larch Av. *CW2: Basf* 2D **48**
Larch Cl. *CW8: Weav* 6H **7**
Larch Rd. *CW2: Crewe* 3E **41**
Larch Tree Cl. *CW8: Barn* 1D **8**
Larkspur Cl. *CW5: Nant* 5G **39**
Latham Rd. *CW11: Sandb* 4C **32**
Latham St. *CW7: Wins* 2E **23**
Latimer Dr. *CW2: Crewe* 1G **41**
Launceston Cl. *CW7: Wins* 4D **22**
Laura St. *CW2: Crewe* 4B **42**
Laurel Bank *CW1: Nort* 3F **23**
Laurel Cl. *CW8: Barn* 1C **8**
CW10: Midd 1H **25**
CW11: Sandb 4E **33**
Laurel Dr. *CW2: Crewe* 3F **41**
Laureston Av. *CW1: Crewe* 1D **42**
Lavender Dr. *CW9: Rudh* 1E **17**
Lavister Cl. *CW9: Nort* 3H **15**
Lawford Cl. *CW1: Crewe* 3F **35**
Lawnsdale *CW8: Cudd* 2B **12**
Lawrence Av. *CW9: Moul* 1G **19**
CW10: Midd 2A **26**
Lawrence Av. E. *CW10: Midd* 2A **26**
Lawrence Cl. *CW4: Cran* 1C **28**
CW11: Elw 3H **31**
Lawrence St. *CW1: Crewe* 1A **42**
Lawton St. *CW2: Crewe* 2A **42**
Lawton Way *CW11: Sandb* 1A **32**
Laxton Way *CW10: Midd* 1A **26**
Lea Av. *CW1: Crewe* 1D **42**
Lea Cl. *CW11: Sandb* 4E **33**
Lea Dr. *CW5: Nant* 3E **45**
Leadsmithy St. *CW10: Midd* 2A **26**
Leaf Gro. *CW7: Wins* 2D **22**
Leaf La. *CW7: Wins* 1A **24**
Leafy Way *CW8: Weav* 6H **7**
Lear Dr. *CW2: Wist* 5F **41**
Lea's Pas. *CW10: Midd* 2H **25**
Leawood Cl. *CW8: Hart* 1C **14**
Ledbury Dr. *CW2: Wist* 6G **41**
Ledward St. *CW7: Wins* 1A **24**
Lee Dr. *CW8: Nort* 1G **15**
LEFTWICH .2A **16**
Leicester St. *CW9: Nort* 4H **9**
Leigh La. *CW8: Lit L* 1G **7**
Leighs Brow *CW8: Barn* 2B **8**
LEIGHTON HOSPITAL 2E **35**
Leighton St. *CW1: Crewe* 6H **35**
Leighton Vw. *CW1: Crewe* 3G **35**
Leigh Way *CW8: Weav* 4G **7**
Leslie Rd. *CW7: Wins* 4C **22**
Leven Av. *CW7: Wins* 1H **23**
Lewin St. *CW10: Midd* 2A **26**
Lewis Cl. *CW5: Nant* 2A **46**
Lewis St. *CW2: Crewe* 2H **41**
Leyland Cl. *CW1: Hasl* 1G **43**
Leyland Wlk. *CW7: Wins* 5E **23**
Lichfield Ct. *CW7: Wins* 4F **23**
Lichfield St. *CW10: Midd* 1B **26**
Lift La. *CW9: And* 2F **9**
Lightley Cl. *CW11: Sandb* 5C **32**
Lightley Ct. *CW11: Sandb* 5C **32**
Lilac Dr. *CW8: Nort* 1F **15**
Lime Av. *CW8: Weav* 5G **7**
CW9: Nort 1H **15**
CW11: Sandb 2C **32**
Lime Cl. *CW10: Midd* 1H **25**
Lime Ct. *CW9: Nort* 2H **15**
Lime Gro. *CW2: Shav* 3A **48**
CW7: Wins 2A **24**
Lime St. *CW1: Hasl* 1G **43**
CW1: Crewe 5A **36**
Lime Tree Av. *CW1: Crewe* 5B **36**
Lime Tree Cl. *CW7: Wins* 3E **23**
Limewood Cres. *CW8: Barn* 1D **8**
Limewood Gro. *CW8: Barn* 1D **8**
Lincoln Cl. *CW1: Crewe* 6H **35**
Linden Ct. *CW1: Crewe* 2C **42**
CW11: Sandb 6B **32**

Linden Dr.—Meadowside

Linden Dr. CW1: Crewe .1D **42**
Lindisfarne Cl. CW10: Midd .2H **25**
Lindsay Wlk. CW8: Cudd .3E **13**
Lingfield Dr. CW1: Crewe .4A **36**
Lingmell Gdns. CW4: Holm C .3B **28**
Linnards La. CW9: Winc .6F **5**
Linnet Cl. CW1: Crewe .4G **35**
CW7: Wins .3A **24**
Linton Ct. CW7: Wins .6A **20**
Linwood CW7: Wins .3B **24**
Lion Salt Works .2C **10**
Lister Cl. CW10: Midd .5B **26**
Littledales La. CW8: Gors, Hart .2H **13**
Lit. Lakes CW2: West .5G **49**
LITTLE LEIGH .1H **7**
LITTLER .2C **22**
Littler Grange Ct.
CW7: Wins .2C **22**
Littler La. CW7: Wins .3B **22**
(not continuous)
Littleton Cl. CW9: Nort .3H **15**
Liverpool St. CW9: Nort .5C **10**
Livingstone Way CW10: Midd .5B **26**
Llandovery Cl. CW7: Wins .4D **22**
Lochleven Rd. CW2: Wist .6G **41**
Lochmaben Cl. CW4: Holm C .4D **28**
Lockerbie Cl. CW4: Holm C .4E **29**
Lockitt St. CW2: Crewe .2B **42**
Locks, The CW10: Midd .3B **26**
Lodge Dr. CW7: Wins .2A **24**
CW9: Moul .2H **19**
Lodgefields Dr. CW2: Crewe .1D **40**
Lodge La. CW8: Hart .3D **14**
CW9: L Gral .3G **11**
CW10: Midd .3E **27**
Lodge Rd. CW11: Sandb .4A **32**
Lomax Rd. CW5: Will .1D **46**
London Rd. CW4: Holm C .3E **29**
CW5: Nant .2H **45**
(not continuous)
CW5: Stap .4B **46**
CW9: Dave .3H **15**
CW9: Nort .5H **9**
CW11: Elw, Sandb .1H **31**
Long Acre CW8: Cudd .3B **12**
CW8: Weav .4G **7**
Longcross Ct. *CW10: Midd .2A 26*
(off Lewin St.)
Longford St. CW2: Crewe .3B **42**
Longhorn Cl. CW10: Midd .1B **26**
Long La. CW10: Midd .3A **26**
Long La. Sth. CW10: Midd .4A **26**
Longmeadow CW8: Weav .4G **7**
Longmoss Cl. CW10: Midd .3H **25**
Longmynd Ri. CW7: Wins .3D **22**
Longwood Cl. CW10: Midd .4A **26**
Loont, The CW7: Wins .4E **23**
Lordsmill Rd. CW2: Shav .3H **47**
Lord St. CW2: Crewe .2B **42**
Lostock Cl. CW9: Nort .2G **15**
LOSTOCK GRALAM .2G **11**
Lostock Gralam Station (Rail) .3G **11**
LOSTOCK GREEN .5G **11**
Lostock Hollow CW9: L Gral, L Gre .4G **11**
Love La. CW5: Nant .2G **45**
Lovell Ct. CW4: Holm C .3E **29**
Lwr. Darwin St. CW8: Nort .1G **15**
Lwr. Haigh St. CW7: Wins .3E **23**
Ludford St. CW1: Crewe .6A **36**
Ludlow Av. CW1: Crewe .2C **42**
Ludlow Cl. CW7: Wins .4D **22**
Lulworth Cl. CW7: Wins .4D **22**
Lunt Av. CW2: Crewe .3H **41**
Lyceum Cl. CW1: Crewe .3G **35**
Lyceum Theatre
Crewe .1B **42**
Lyceum Way CW1: Crewe .3G **35**
Lydgate Cl. CW2: Wist .5F **41**
Lydyett La. CW8: Barn .2D **8**
Lymcote Dr. CW8: Hart .3C **14**
Lynbrook Rd. CW1: Crewe .1D **42**
Lyncroft Cl. CW1: Crewe .2D **42**
Lyndale Ct. CW7: Wins .6A **20**
Lynton Gro. CW1: Hasl .6H **37**
Lynton Way CW2: Wist .5G **41**
Lyon St. CW1: Crewe .1B **42**
Lytham Dr. CW7: Wins .1E **23**

M

Mablins La. CW1: Crewe .3H **35**
Macclesfield Rd. CW4: Holm C .3E **29**
McLaren St. CW1: Crewe .4H **35**
McNeill Av. CW1: Crewe .6F **35**
Macon Ct. CW1: Crewe .2C **42**
Macon Ind. Pk. CW1: Crewe .2C **42**
Macon Way CW1: Crewe .2C **42**
Madeley St. CW2: Crewe .4A **42**
Magdala Pl. CW9: Nort .5C **10**
Magdalen Ct. CW2: Crewe .4G **41**
Magecroft CW1: Leig .2H **35**
Maidenhills CW10: Midd .3B **26**
Maidwell Cl. CW7: Wins .5A **20**
Main Rd. CW1: Crewe, Warm .6B **30**
CW2: Shav .4G **47**
CW2: West .6G **43**
CW5: Worl .5G **39** & 6A **34**
CW5: Wyb .6G **47**
CW9: Moul .1G **19**
Mainwaring Cl. CW5: Stap .3A **46**
Maisterson Ct. CW5: Nant .2G **45**
Maitland-Wood Cl. CW9: Nort .6D **10**
Malam Dr. CW9: Rudh .1D **16**
Malbank CW5: Nant .1G **45**
Malbank Rd. CW2: Crewe .1D **40**
MALKIN'S BANK .6E **33**
Mallaig Cl. CW4: Holm C .5E **29**
Mallard Ct. CW1: Crewe .3E **43**
Mallard Way CW1: Crewe .3E **43**
CW7: Wins .5F **23**
Malmesbury Cl. CW10: Midd .2H **25**
Malory Cl. CW1: Crewe .6D **36**
Malpas Cl. CW9: Nort .6C **10**
Malpas Rd. CW9: Nort .5B **10**
Malt Kiln Way CW11: Sandb .2D **32**
Malvern Cl. CW2: Shav .3H **47**
Malvern Way CW7: Wins .4D **22**
Manchester Metropolitan University Cheshire
Crewe Campus .2D **42**
Manchester Rd. CW9: L Gral, Nort .4B **10**
Manifold Cl. CW11: Sandb .1A **32**
Manley Cl. CW4: Holm C .3C **28**
CW9: Nort .2A **16**
Manning St. CW2: Crewe .4B **42**
Manora Rd. CW9: Nort .5A **10**
Manor Av. CW2: Crewe .4G **41**
CW9: Mars .5B **4**
Manor Ct. CW2: Crewe .4H **41**
CW5: Edle .4D **44**
CW5: Nant .1G 45
(off Cowfields)
Manor Cres. CW10: Midd .4A **26**
Manor Dr. CW8: Barn .3D **8**
CW9: Nort .6C **10**
Manor Flds. CW10: Midd .4A **26**
Manor Gdns. *CW5: Nant .1G 45*
(off Manor Rd.)
Manor Gro. CW8: Nort .1E **15**
Manor La. CW4: Holm C .4F **29**
CW9: What .4D **16**
CW10: Midd .3A **26**
MANOR PARK .4H **25**
Manor Rd. CW5: Nant .1G **45**
CW8: Cudd .5D **12**
CW11: Sandb .3F **33**
Manor Rd. Nth. CW5: Nant .6G **39**
Manor Sq. CW7: Wins .3C **22**
Manor St. CW8: Nort .1F **15**
Manor Way CW2: Crewe .4H **41**
CW11: Sandb .3G **33**
Maple Cl. CW4: Holm C .2F **29**
CW11: Sandb .3E **33**
Maple Gro. CW1: Crewe .4C **36**
CW7: Wins .2A **24**
CW8: Barn .1D **8**
CW8: Nort .6E **9**
Maple La. CW8: Cudd .5D **12**
Maples, The CW7: Wins .6A **20**
Marbury Country Pk. .6G **3**
Marbury La. CW9: Marb, Mars .6F **3**
Marbury Rd. CW9: And .1F **9**
CW9: Comb .4F **3**
March St. CW1: Crewe .1C **42**
Mardale Ct. CW4: Holm C .4C **28**
Marford Cl. CW9: Nort .2G **15**
Marine App. CW8: Nort .5H **9**
Market Arc. *CW9: Nort .5H 9*
(off Watling St.)
Market Cen. CW1: Crewe .1B **42**
Market Cl. CW1: Crewe .6B **36**
Market Pl. CW7: Wins .2H **23**
Market Sq. CW1: Crewe .1B **42**
CW11: Sandb .3D **32**
Market St. CW1: Crewe .1B **42**
(Chantry Ct.)
CW1: Crewe .6B **36**
(Vernon Way)
CW5: Nant .2G **45**
CW9: Nort .5H **9**
Market Way *CW9: Nort .5H 9*
(off Market St.)
Marlborough Av. CW7: Wins .6E **19**
Marlborough Cl. CW2: Wist .5E **41**
Marlborough Dr. CW11: Sandb .1D **32**
Marl Cl. CW8: Cudd .3E **13**
Marley Av. CW1: Crewe .4H **35**
Marlow Cl. CW11: Etti H .4H **31**
Marlowe Cl. CW2: Wist .5G **41**
Marlowe Dr. CW5: Nant .4G **45**
Marlowe Rd. CW9: Nort .6C **10**
Marple Cres. CW2: Crewe .3E **41**
Marple Rd. CW9: Nort .6C **10**
Marriott Rd. CW11: Sandb .6B **32**
Marshall La. CW8: Nort .1E **15**
Marshalls Arm Nature Reserve .2F **15**
Marshalls Ct. CW8: Hart .2E **15**
Marshfield Av. CW2: Crewe .6D **34**
MARSHFIELD BANK .1D **40**
Marshfield Bank CW2: Crewe .1D **40**
Marsh Grn. Rd. CW11: Elw, Sandb .1H **31**
Marsh La. CW4: Holm C .4F **29**
CW5: Act, Edle, Rave .5A **44**
CW5: Nant .3E **45**
CW8: Crow .5A **6**
MARSTON .2C **10**
Marston La. CW9: Mars, Winc .5B **4**
Marton Cl. CW2: Hou .4C **48**
MARTON SANDS .5A **18**
Martree Ct. CW11: Elw .1H **31**
Marys Ga. CW2: Wist .5E **41**
Mary St. CW1: Crewe .6C **36**
Masefield Dr. CW1: Crewe .1D **42**
Masefield Way CW11: Etti H .4H **31**
Massey Av. CW7: Wins .2H **23**
CW8: Hart .3C **14**
Massey Cl. CW5: Stap .3A **46**
Mather Cl. CW10: Midd .3A **26**
Mather Dr. CW9: Comb .4E **3**
CW9: Nort .6D **10**
Mavor Ct. CW1: Crewe .1A **42**
MAW GREEN .4C **36**
Maw Grn. Cl. CW1: Crewe .4C **36**
Maw Grn. Rd. CW1: Crewe .4C **36**
Maw La. CW1: Crewe, Hasl .4E **37**
Maxwell St. CW2: Crewe .2A **42**
Mayfair Dr. CW1: Crewe .5D **36**
CW9: Nort .4G **15**
Mayfield Cl. CW4: Holm C .3F **29**
Mayfield Dr. CW7: Wins .6H **19**
CW8: Cudd .3E **13**
Mayfield Gro. CW8: Cudd .3E **13**
Mayfield M. CW1: Crewe .5F **35**
Mayfield Rd. CW9: Nort .5C **10**
Mayflower Rd. CW5: Nant .4G **45**
Meadow Av. CW2: West .2F **49**
MEADOWBANK .4G **19**
Meadow Cl. CW2: Shav .2B **48**
CW7: Wins .6E **19**
CW8: Cudd .3E **13**
Meadow Dr. CW2: Wist .6F **41**
CW8: Barn .2C **8**
Meadow Ga. CW9: Winc .6F **5**
Meadowgate Cl. CW11: Etti H .4H **31**
Meadow Gro. CW7: Wins .4G **19**
CW9: Nort .2A **16**
Meadow Home Pk. CW7: Whit .3F **19**
Meadow La. CW9: Comb .4E **3**
CW9: Moul .2H **19**
Meadow Ri. CW7: Wins .2C **22**
Meadow Rd. CW8: Weav .5A **8**
Meadowside CW8: Nort .6F **9**

60 A-Z Crewe

Meadow St. CW9: Nort 4A 10
Meadowvale Cl. CW5: Nant 6G 39
Meadow Vw. CW10: Midd 1H 25
Medina Av. CW7: Wins 1H 23
Meeanee Dr. CW5: Nant 3E 45
Melbourne Gro. CW1: Hasl 6G 37
Melchett Cres. CW9: Rudh 6D 10
Melford Cl. CW2: Wist 5A 42
Mellor St. CW1: Crewe 6B 36
Melrose Dr. CW1: Crewe 3H 35
Mendip Cl. CW7: Wins 3D 22
Mercer Way CW5: Nant 6G 39
Merchants Ct. CW1: Crewe 4A 36
Mercian Cl. CW2: Shav 3H 47
Mere Bank CW9: Dave 1A 20
Merebank Rd. CW2: Crewe 4H 41
Mere Brook Wlk. CW2: Crewe 5A 42
Mere Cl. CW1: Hasl 1H 43
  WA16: Pick 4G 5
Mere Ct. CW2: West 2F 49
Meredith St. CW1: Crewe 6A 36
Merehaven Cl. WA16: Pick 4F 5
MERE HEATH 1A 20
Mere La. CW8: Cudd, Sandi 5E 13
  WA16: Pick 5F 5
Mere Rd. CW2: West 2F 49
  CW9: Mars 5B 4
Mere St. CW1: Hasl 1H 43
Mere Vw. Cvn. Pk. WA16: Pick 5F 5
Mereworth Dr. CW9: Nort 2H 15
Merlin Cl. CW7: Wins 3A 24
Merlin Ct. CW1: Crewe 3G 35
Merlin Way CW1: Crewe 3G 35
Merrill's Av. CW2: Crewe 6E 35
Merrivale Rd. CW2: Wist 5G 41
Mersey Pl. CW7: Wins 2B 24
  (off Trent Av.)
Mervyn Rd. CW8: Weav 4A 8
Mews, The CW4: Holm C 3E 29
  CW8: Barn 3D 8
Meynell Cl. CW2: Wist 4G 41
Micklewright Av. CW1: Crewe 6B 36
Middlehurst Av. CW8: Weav 5A 8
MIDDLEWICH 3A 26
Middlewich Leisure Cen. 3A 26
Middlewich Rd.
  CW1: Brad G, Crewe, Leig, Wool ..5A 40
  CW1: Leig 4E 35
  CW2: Crewe, Nant, Wist, Wool ..5A 40
  CW4: Holm C 3A 28
  CW5: Nant, Will, Wist 6G 39
  CW7: Wins 2C 24
  CW9: Nort 5B 10
  CW10: Stan 2C 24
  CW11: Sandb 2A 32
Middlewich St. CW1: Crewe 4B 36
Midpoint 18 Motorway Ind. Est.
  CW10: Midd 2C 26
Millbeck Cl. CW2: West 2F 49
Millbri. Cl. CW1: Crewe 2D 42
Millbrook Cl. CW7: Wins 3B 22
Millbrook Ct. CW10: Midd 2B 26
Millbuck Pk. CW11: Etti H 4G 31
Millbuck Way CW11: Etti H 3H 31
  (not continuous)
Millennium Ga. CW1: Crewe 3D 42
Milley La. WA16: Pick 3H 5
Millfields CW5: Nant 2F 45
Millgate CW8: Cudd 3D 12
Mill Hill Dr. CW11: Sandb 4C 32
Mill Hill La. CW11: Sandb 4C 32
Milling Fld., The CW4: Holm C 4E 29
Millington La. CW8: Gors 1E 13
Mill La. CW2: West 1E 49
  CW4: Holm C 4G 29
  CW7: Wins 2C 18
  CW8: Cudd 2D 12
  CW8: Whit 2C 18
  CW10: Midd 2A 26
  (Kinderton St.)
  CW10: Midd 2H 25
  (Tewkesbury Cl.)
  CW11: Hass, Malk B, Whee 6C 32
  (not continuous)
  CW11: Most 1G 31
Millrace Dr. CW2: Wist 5H 41
Mill Row CW11: Sandb 3E 33

Millstone La. CW5: Nant 1H 45
Mill St. CW2: Crewe 2B 42
  CW5: Nant 2G 45
Mills Way CW1: Leig 2H 35
Mill Way CW5: Nant 5H 45
Millwood Dr. CW8: Hart 3A 14
Milne Cl. CW2: Wist 4F 41
Milner Rd. CW8: Nort 1E 15
Milton Cl. CW9: Winc 6G 5
  CW10: Midd 6B 26
Milton Dr. CW2: Wist 5F 41
Milton Rough CW8: Act B 3C 6
Milton Way CW11: Etti H 3H 31
Minshull New Rd. CW1: Crewe 5F 35
Minster Cl. CW7: Wins 6F 23
Minster Cl. CW2: Wist 5E 41
Mirion St. CW1: Crewe 1B 42
Moat Ho. Dr. CW2: Crewe 3G 41
Moat, The (Nature Reserve) 2F 31
Model Cotts. CW4: Cran 1C 28
Monarch Cl. CW2: Crewe 1F 41
Monarch Dr. CW9: Nort 2G 15
Monck Dr. CW5: Nant 1F 45
Mond St. CW8: Barn 3D 8
Monks La. CW1: Crewe 5F 35
  CW5: Act 6A 38
  CW5: Nant 2G 45
  (off Dysart Bldgs.)
Monks Orchard CW5: Nant 2H 45
Monk St. CW1: Crewe 6G 35
Monks Way CW8: Hart 3D 14
Montgomery Way CW7: Wins 4D 22
Montrose Cl. CW2: Shav 4H 47
Montrose Ct. CW4: Holm C 4D 28
Moorfields CW5: Will 1E 47
Moorings, The CW10: Midd 2A 26
Moorlands Av. CW8: Cudd 3E 13
Moorlands Dr. CW5: Wyb 6G 47
  (not continuous)
Moorlands Pk. CW8: Cudd 3E 13
Moor-Park Way CW9: Nort 3H 15
Moors La. CW7: Darn, Wins 6E 23
Moreton Cl. CW11: Sandb 2E 33
Moreton Dr. CW4: Holm C 3D 28
Moreton Rd. CW2: Crewe 3F 41
Moreton's Meade CW8: Weav 6A 8
Moreton St. CW8: Winn 4F 9
Moreville Cl. CW9: Nort 3G 15
Morgan Cl. CW2: Crewe 1G 41
Morgan Wlk. CW5: Nant 1F 45
  (off Water-Lode)
Mornant Av. CW8: Hart 3B 14
Mornington Cl. CW11: Elw 2H 31
Morris Dr. CW8: Weav 4H 7
Morris Pk. CW8: Hart 3D 14
Mortimer Dr. CW11: Sandb 4E 33
Moss, The CW9: Comb 4F 3
Moss Bank CW7: Wins 2D 22
  CW8: Winn 5F 9
Moss Bri. CW11: Most 2G 31
Moss Cft. CW1: Crewe 3G 35
Mossdale Cl. CW2: Crewe 1E 41
Moss Dr. CW10: Midd 5B 26
Moss Farm Recreation Cen. 5F 9
Moss Flds. CW1: Crewe 2G 35
Mossford Av. CW1: Crewe 4H 35
MOSS LANE 2D 4
Moss La. CW1: Brad G, Leig, Mins V ..1E 35
  CW1: Warm 6A 30
  CW5: Wyb 6G 47
  CW7: Wins 2D 24
  CW8: Cudd 4D 12
  CW8: Winn 6F 9
  (not continuous)
  CW9: Mars, Winc 5E 5
  CW11: Elw 2G 31
Moss La. Bus. Cen. CW11: Etti H ..3H 31
Moss La. Ind. Est. CW11: Elw 2H 31
Moss Rd. CW8: Winn 4F 9
Moss Sq. CW1: Crewe 1B 42
Moss St. CW8: Weav 4H 7
Moss Ter. CW8: Winn 4E 9
MOSTON GREEN 1E 31
Moston Rd. CW11: Etti H 4G 31
Mottram Cl. CW10: Midd 4H 25
Mottram Dr. CW5: Nant 3H 45
Mouldsworth Cl. CW9: Nort 3G 15

MOULTON 1H 19
Moulton Cl. CW9: Nort 3G 15
Mount, The CW9: Gt B 4A 4
Mountbatten Cl. CW2: Crewe 2G 41
Mount Cl. CW5: Nant 1H 45
Mount Dr. CW5: Nant 1H 45
Mt. Pleasant CW1: Crewe 5H 35
  CW1: Hasl 1H 43
Mt. Pleasant Dr. CW1: Crewe 4C 22
Mt. Pleasant Rd. CW9: Dave 5H 15
Muirfield Cl. CW9: Nort 2A 16
Muirfield Dr. CW7: Wins 1E 23
Muirfield M. CW7: Wins 1E 23
  (off Buttermere Rd.)
Mulberry Gdns. CW11: Elw 2H 31
Mulberry Ri. CW8: Nort 6E 9
Mulberry Rd. CW2: Crewe 3E 41
Mulcaster Ct. CW1: Hasl 6H 37
Murrayfield Dr. CW5: Will 2D 46
Myrtle St. CW2: Crewe 2A 42
Mytton Dr. CW5: Nant 1F 45

N

Nairn Av. CW4: Holm C 4D 28
NANTWICH 2G 45
Nantwich Mus. 2G 45
Nantwich Players Theatre 2G 45
Nantwich Rd. CW1: Crewe 4H 41
  CW2: Crewe 4H 41
  CW10: Midd, Stan, Wimb 5F 25
Nantwich Station (Rail) 3G 45
Nantwich Swimming Pool & Fitness Cen.
  ....1F 45
Nantwich Tennis Club 5H 39
Narrow La. CW7: Crewe G 2F 43
Nat La. CW7: Wins 6H 19
  (not continuous)
Nat La. Bus. Pk. CW7: Wins 6H 19
Nat La. Retail Pk. CW7: Wins 1H 23
Navan Cl. CW1: Crewe 6H 35
  (off Richard St.)
Navigation Rd. CW8: Nort 6H 9
Naylor Ct. CW9: Nort 5H 9
Naylor Cres. CW5: Stap 3A 46
Needham Dr. CW4: Cran 1C 28
  CW8: Hart 3C 14
Needhams Bank CW11: Most 3G 31
Nelson St. CW2: Crewe 3A 42
Nessina Gro. CW2: Wist 5F 41
Neumann St. CW9: Nort 5B 10
Neville St. CW2: Crewe 4B 42
Nevis Dr. CW2: Crewe 2D 40
Newall Av. CW11: Sandb 4C 32
Newall Cres. CW7: Wins 2A 24
Newbold Way CW5: Nant 4G 45
Newbury Av. CW1: Crewe 4A 36
  CW7: Wins 3C 22
Newcastle Rd. CW2: Chor, Hou, Shav ..4A 48
  CW5: Bla, Stap, Will 3B 46
  CW11: Blet 5H 33
Newcastle St. CW1: Crewe 6G 35
Newdigate St. CW1: Crewe 6A 36
  (not continuous)
Newfield Dr. CW1: Crewe 6C 36
Newfield St. CW11: Sandb 2D 32
Newhaven Ct. CW5: Nant 2H 45
New King St. CW10: Midd 1A 26
Newland Way CW5: Stap 3B 46
New La. CW7: Darn 6H 23
New Rd. CW7: Wins 1G 23
  CW9: And 2E 9
New Rd. Bus. Cen. CW7: Wins 1G 23
New St. CW1: Hasl 6G 37
  CW11: Elw 2H 31
Newton Bank CW10: Midd 2H 25
Newton Hall M. CW10: Midd 3A 26
Newton Heath CW10: Midd 2H 25
NEWTONIA 3H 25
Newton St. CW1: Crewe 6A 36
New Warrington Rd.
  CW9: Mars, Nort, Winc 4B 10
Nicholas Av. CW9: Rudh 1C 16
Nicholas Rd. CW8: Weav 4H 7
Niddries La. CW9: Moul 2G 19
Nigel Gresley Cl. CW1: Crewe 1E 43

Nightingale Cl. CW10: Midd 5B 26
Nightingale Ct. CW7: Wins 5F 23
Nile St. CW2: Crewe 3A 42
Nixon Dr. CW7: Wins 1C 22
Nixon Rd. CW8: Cudd 4D 12
Nixons Row CW5: Nant 2E 45
Nixon St. CW1: Crewe 6F 35
Norbreck Av. CW2: Crewe 3H 41
Norbury Cl. CW2: Hou 4C 48
Norbury Dr. CW10: Midd 3H 25
Norbury St. CW9: Nort 5B 10
Norley Pl. CW9: Nort 2G 15
Norley Rd. CW8: Cudd 3A 12
   CW8: Cudd, Sandi 3B 12
   WA6: Cudd .3A 12
Norman Dr. CW7: Wins 5E 23
Normandy Av. CW7: Wins 3F 23
Northbank Wlk. *CW2: Crewe* *5A 42*
   (off Artle Rd.)
North Crofts CW5: Nant 2G 45
North Dr. CW9: Rudh 6E 11
Northfield Pl. CW2: Shav 2A 48
Nth. Stafford St. CW1: Crewe 1B 42
North St. CW1: Crewe 4A 36
North Vw. CW1: Crewe 5G 35
Northway CW7: Shav 2B 48
   CW4: Holm C 3E 29
   CW8: Winn .4F 9
NORTHWICH **5H 9**
Northwich Retail Pk. CW9: Nort 4C 10
Northwich Rd. CW8: Hart, Weav 4G 7
   CW9: Antr, Gt B, Mars 1D 2
Northwich Station (Rail) **5B 10**
Northwich Victoria FC **2D 10**
Northwood Av. CW10: Midd 6C 26
Norton Way CW11: Elw 2H 31
Nova Ct. *CW1: Crewe* *6H 35*
   (off Dewes St.)
Nun Ho. Cl. CW7: Wins 2B 24
Nun Ho. Dr. CW7: Wins 2B 24
Nunsmere Cl. CW7: Wins 2B 24
Nursery, The CW8: Hart 1E 15
Nursery Cl. CW2: Crewe 3G 41
   CW2: Shav .4A 48
Nursery Rd. CW8: Barn 2D 8
Nutfield Av. CW1: Crewe 4H 35
Nuthurst Gdns. CW5: Nant 2H 45

O

Oak Av. CW7: Wins 4F 23
Oak Bank Cl. CW5: Will 3E 47
Oakdale Cl. CW2: West 5F 49
Oakdene Ct. CW11: Sandb 3D 32
Oak Dr. CW10: Midd 4B 26
Oakfield Ri. CW4: Holm C 3D 28
Oak Gro. CW5: Nant 4G 45
Oakhouse La. CW7: Wins 3D 22
   (not continuous)
Oakhurst Dr. CW2: Wist 6H 41
Oakland Av. CW1: Hasl 1G 43
Oaklands Ct. *CW2: Eng B* *4H 49*
   (off Golden Hill)
Oak La. CW8: Cudd 5D 12
Oakleigh Ri. CW8: Winn 4G 9
Oakley Cl. CW11: Sandb 1C 32
Oakley St. CW1: Crewe 6A 36
Oak Mdw. CW8: Weav 6A 8
Oakmere Cl. CW11: Sandb 2B 32
Oakmere Hall CW8: Oak 6C 12
Oakmere Pl. *CW1: Crewe* *6H 35*
   (off Rigg St.)
Oakmere Rd. CW7: Wins 1B 22
Oak St. CW2: Crewe 2B 42
   CW9: Nort .4A 10
   CW11: Sandb 1H 31
Oak Tree Cl. CW1: Crewe 6D 36
   CW8: Barn .1D 8
Oak Tree Dr. CW1: Crewe 6D 36
Oakwood Cl. CW8: Barn 3C 8
Oakwood Cres. CW2: Crewe 1E 41
   CW11: Sandb 3G 33
Oakwood Ho. *CW8: Barn* *3C 8*
   (off Blackcroft Av.)
Oakwood La. CW8: Barn 3C 8
   CW11: Most 1F 31

Oat Mkt. CW5: Nant 2G 45
Oddfellows Pas. *CW10: Midd* *2H 25*
   (off Chester Rd.)
Offley Av. CW11: Sandb 2D 32
Offley Rd. CW11: Sandb 2D 32
Old Applecroft CW11: Etti H 4G 31
Oldfield Rd. CW11: Sandb 5B 32
Old Gate Cl. CW10: Midd 4H 25
Old Gorse Cl. CW2: Crewe 2E 41
Old Hall Gdns. CW11: Sandb 3D 32
Old Hall Rd. CW9: Nort 2A 16
Oldhams Hill CW8: Nort 4H 9
Old La. CW8: Act B 3C 6
   CW9: Antr .1E 3
   CW9: What .5D 16
Old Middlewich Rd. *CW11: Sandb* *3D 32*
   (off Hightown)
Old Mill La. WA4: High W 1A 2
Old Mill Rd. CW11: Sandb 3D 32
Old Newcastle Rd. CW5: Will 3D 46
Old Orchard, The CW8: Cudd 3D 12
Old Park Rd. CW1: Crewe 6H 43
Old Rd. CW9: And 2F 9
Old School Cl. CW8: Barn 3D 8
Old Vicarage La. CW8: Hart 2E 15
Old Warrington Rd. CW9: Mars, Nort 4A 10
Ollershaw La. CW9: Mars 5C 4
ONSTON **4C 6**
Onston La. CW8: Crow 4C 6
Orchard Av. CW8: Act B 1C 6
Orchard Cl. CW7: Wins 4F 23
   CW8: Barn .2D 8
   CW8: Weav .4H 7
   CW8: Winc .5G 5
   CW10: Midd 4B 26
Orchard Ct. CW1: Hasl 6H 37
Orchard Cres. CW5: Nant 4G 45
Orchard Dene CW8: Cudd 2B 12
Orchard Dr. CW8: Lit L 1H 7
Orchard Gdns. CW8: Weav 4F 7
Orchard Ri. CW9: Moul 1G 19
Orchards, The CW2: Shav 3A 48
   WA16: Pick .5F 5
Orchard St. CW1: Crewe 6A 36
   CW5: Will 1D 46
   CW9: Nort .5B 10
Ordsall Cl. CW11: Sandb 6B 32
Orion Way CW1: Crewe 3F 43
Ormerod Cl. CW11: Sandb 4E 33
Orton Cl. CW7: Wins 5A 20
Osborne Cl. CW11: Etti H 4H 31
Osborne Gro. CW2: Shav 3H 47
Osprey Av. CW7: Wins 6E 23
Osprey Cl. CW10: Midd 6B 26
Ossmere Cl. CW11: Sandb 1B 32
Otters Bank CW7: Wins 2C 22
Ousel Nest CW8: Cudd 3B 12
OVER **4D 22**
Overdale La. CW8: Oak 6B 12
Overdene Rd. CW7: Wins 3F 23
Over Hall Dr. CW7: Wins 4E 23
Over Sq. CW7: Wins 3D 22
Overton Cl. CW10: Midd 3H 25
Overway CW7: Wins 2G 23
Owen St. CW2: Crewe 3A 42
   CW9: Nort .5B 10
Owley Wood Rd. CW8: Weav 4A 8
Oxford St. CW1: Crewe 6H 35

P

Paddock, The CW5: Will 3D 46
   CW8: Hart .4E 15
   CW11: Sandb 2D 32
Paddock Vw. CW10: Midd 1A 26
Paddock Wlk. CW8: Cudd 2B 12
Padmore Cl. CW1: Crewe 4G 35
Padstow Cl. CW1: Crewe 3A 36
Padworth Pl. CW1: Leig 2H 35
Page Gro. CW2: Shav 4H 47
Pall Mall CW5: Nant 2G 45
Palmer Cl. CW9: Nort 2H 15
Palmer Rd. CW11: Sandb 3E 33
Palmerston Cl. CW1: Hasl 6G 37
Park Av. CW7: Wins 6A 20
   CW8: Weav .4H 7

Park Cres. CW8: Cudd 3D 12
Park Dr. CW2: Wist 4F 41
Park Dr. Gdns. CW2: Wist 5F 41
Parker Av. CW8: Hart 1C 14
Parker's Rd. CW1: Crewe, Leig 3G 35
Park Est. CW2: Shav 2B 48
Parkfield CW1: Leig 3G 35
Parkfield Dr. CW5: Nant 3G 45
Parkfield Rd. CW9: Nort 5B 10
Park Ho. Dr. CW11: Sandb 1E 33
Park Ho. M. CW11: Sandb 1F 33
Parklands CW10: Midd 4H 25
Parklands Dr. CW2: Eng B 4H 49
Parkland Vw. CW5: Nant 3F 45
Park La. CW8: Hart 3D 14
   CW9: Ast B, Pick 3C 4
   CW9: Moul .2H 19
   CW11: Sandb 3B 32
   WA16: Pick .4F 5
Park Mills Cl. CW5: Will 2D 46
Park Rd. CW1: Hasl 6H 37
   CW5: Nant .4G 45
   CW5: Will 1C 46
   CW8: Winn .4F 9
   CW10: Midd 2A 26
Parkstone Dr. CW1: Crewe 3H 35
Park St. CW8: Nort 6G 9
Park Vw. CW1: Hasl 1H 43
   CW5: Nant .1H 45
Parkway CW4: Holm C 3E 29
Parliament St. CW8: Nort 6F 9
Partridge Cl. CW7: Wins 6F 23
Partridge Way CW9: Winc 6F 5
Pastures Cl. CW2: Eng B 3H 49
Patterdale Cl. CW2: Crewe 2D 40
Paulden Rd. CW9: L Gral 3G 11
Pavilions, The CW9: Dave 5G 15
Peach La. CW5: Nant 4A 40
Peacock Av. CW7: Wins 5E 23
Pear Tree Av. CW1: Crewe 4H 35
Pear Tree Cl. CW7: Wins 4F 23
   CW8: Weav .4G 7
Peartree Cl. CW11: Sandb 3G 33
Pear Tree Dr. CW9: Winc 5F 5
Pear Tree Farm Cotts. CW9: Nort 3F 17
Pear Tree Fld. CW5: Stap 3A 46
Pear Tree La. CW8: Act B 1C 6
Peckforton Cl. CW11: Sandb 2A 32
Peckforton Way *CW8: Nort* *6G 9*
   (off Beeston St.)
Pedley St. CW2: Crewe 3B 42
Peebles Cl. CW4: Holm C 4D 28
Peel Sq. *CW1: Crewe* *6H 35*
   (off Cornwall Gro.)
Peel St. CW1: Crewe 6H 35
Peewit Cl. CW7: Wins 6F 23
Pelham Cl. CW1: Hasl 6H 37
Pelican Cl. CW1: Crewe 6E 37
Pembroke Way CW7: Wins 4D 22
Penbrook Cl. CW2: Crewe 2D 40
Penda Way *CW11: Sandb* *3D 32*
   (off Market Sq.)
Pendle Cl. CW1: Crewe 6E 37
Penlington Ct. CW5: Nant 1H 45
Pennine Way CW7: Wins 3D 22
Pennymoor Dr. CW10: Midd 1A 26
Pennys La. CW9: Rudh 6E 11
   (not continuous)
Penrhyn Rd. CW8: Winn 5F 9
Pentland Cl. CW7: Wins 3D 22
Pepper St. CW5: Nant 2G 45
   CW10: Midd 2A 26
Percy St. CW9: Nort 5A 10
Peregrine Cl. CW7: Wins 6F 23
Perry Flds. CW1: Leig 2H 35
Perth Cl. CW4: Holm C 4D 28
Peter Destapleigh Way
   CW5: Nant, Stap 4H 45
Peter Ellson Cl. CW2: Crewe 4B 42
Peter Pl. CW1: Crewe 6H 35
Petersfield Way CW2: Eng B 3H 49
Peter St. CW9: Nort 4B 10
Petrel Cl. CW7: Wins 6F 23
Pettypool Activity Cen. **6F 13**
Petworth Cl. CW7: Wins 5H 41
Pheasant Dr. CW9: Winc 6F 5
Pheasant Way CW7: Wins 6F 23

Phoenix Leisure Pk. 1A 42
Pickering Way CW5: Nant 3H 45
PICKMERE .4F 5
Pickmere Cl. CW11: Sandb 2B 32
Pickmere Ct. CW1: Crewe 6A 36
Pickmere La. CW9: Winc 5F 5
  WA16: Pick 5F 5
Pickwick Cl. CW11: Sandb 1E 33
Picton Cl. CW9: Nort 3H 15
Picton Dr. CW7: Wins 1D 22
Picton Sq. CW4: Holm C 3E 29
Pike, The CW5: Nant 4G 45
Pikenall La. CW8: Act B, Crow 2A 6
Pillory St. CW5: Nant 2G 45
Pineapple Pk. CW7: Wins 1B 24
Pine Gro. CW7: Wins 2A 24
  CW11: Sandb 3E 33
Pine Tree Cl. CW8: Barn 1D 8
Pinetree Cl. CW7: Wins 2A 24
Pine Wlk. CW5: Nant 3H 45
Pinewood Ct. CW2: Wist 6H 41
Pinewood Rd. CW7: Wins 2D 22
Pinfold La. CW10: Midd 2H 25
  (off Newton Bank)
Pinfold Way CW8: Weav 4H 7
Pingard's La. CW8: Crow 5A 6
Pintail Pl. CW7: Wins 5F 23
Pipers Ash CW7: Wins 2C 22
Pippin Cl. CW10: Midd 4A 26
Pit La. CW2: Hou 5C 48
Plane Tree Dr. CW1: Crewe 5C 36
Plantagenet Cl. CW7: Wins 5F 23
Plant La. CW11: Most 1E 31
Plant St. CW11: Sandb 2C 32
Platt Av. CW11: Sandb 2C 32
Pleasant St. CW8: Nort 6G 9
Plover Av. CW7: Wins 6F 23
Plumbs Fold CW8: Barn 3C 8
Pochard Av. CW7: Wins 5F 23
Pochin Way CW10: Midd 2C 26
Points Ho. CW1: Crewe 6G 35
  (off Dale Way)
Pole La. CW9: Antr 2G 3
Pollard Dr. CW5: Stap 3B 46
Poole Hill Rd. CW5: Henh, Poole 4C 38
Poole Old Hall La. CW5: Poole, Worl . . .1E 39
Poole St. CW7: Wins 2G 23
Poolford La. CW4: Spro 1H 27
Pool Mdws. Rd. CW1: Hasl 1F 43
Poor's Wood Nature Reserve 4F 15
Poplar Av. CW9: Moul 1H 19
Poplar Cl. CW7: Wins 3D 22
  CW8: Cudd 4D 12
Poplar Ct. CW5: Stap 3A 46
Poplar Dr. CW10: Midd 4B 26
Poplar Gro. CW1: Crewe 6C 36
Poplar Rd. CW8: Weav 5H 7
Poplars, The CW2: Wist 6F 41
Poppies, The CW9: Moul 1H 19
Poppy Cl. CW2: West 2G 49
Porter Dr. CW9: Nort 1C 16
Porter Way CW9: Nort 1C 16
Portland Dr. CW7: Wins 3D 22
Portland Gro. CW1: Hasl 6G 37
Portman Pl. CW7: Wins 3C 22
  (off Brockwell Cl.)
Portree Dr. CW4: Holm C 4D 28
Postles Pl. CW9: Nort 1H 15
Post Office Pl. CW9: Nort 4A 10
Potter Cl. CW5: Will 3D 46
Pratchitts Row CW5: Nant 2G 45
Precinct, The CW2: Crewe 3F 41
Preece Ct. CW1: Crewe 6H 35
Premier Pk. CW7: Wins 6B 20
Prestbury Cl. CW9: Nort 3H 15
Prestwick Cl. CW7: Wins 1E 23
  (off Gleneagles Dr.)
Price Av. CW11: Sandb 4C 32
Price Dr. CW11: Sandb 4C 32
Priestley Ct. CW5: Nant 2G 45
  (off Hospital St.)
Primrose Av. CW1: Hasl 6G 37
Primrose Hill CW2: Crewe 6E 35
  CW8: Cudd 3D 12
Prince Albert St. CW1: Crewe 1B 42
Prince Edward St. CW5: Nant 1G 45

Princes Av. CW9: Nort 5B 10
Princes Ct. CW5: Nant 6G 39
Princes Pk. CW8: Barn 3C 8
Princess Cl. CW2: Wist 5F 41
Princess Cres. CW10: Midd 5B 26
Princess Dr. CW5: Nant 5F 41
  CW5: Nant 1A 46
  CW11: Sandb 1C 32
Princess Gro. CW2: Wist 5F 41
Princess St. CW1: Crewe 5A 36
  CW7: Wins 2A 24
  CW9: Nort 3E 11
Prior Cl. CW2: Wist 4F 41
Priory Av. CW9: Nort 3H 15
Priory Cl. CW1: Crewe 3G 35
  CW7: Wins 6E 19
Priory St. CW9: Nort 5A 10
Priory Way CW8: Hart 3D 14
Priscilla St. CW1: Crewe 1C 42
Pritchard Dr. CW9: Dave 5G 15
Probert Cl. CW2: Crewe 1G 41
Proctors La. CW11: Etti H 4H 31
Prospect Dr. CW9: Dave 5G 15
Prosperity Way CW10: Midd 2B 26
Prunus Rd. CW1: Crewe 5B 36
Ptarmigan Pl. CW7: Wins 6F 23
Pulford Cl. CW9: Nort 3G 15
Pulford Rd. CW7: Wins 2E 23
Pullman Dr. CW9: Nort 5C 10
Pym's La. CW1: Crewe, Wool 5D 34
  CW2: Wool 5D 34
Pyrus Av. CW1: Crewe 5C 36

Q

Quaintways CW8: Hart 3E 15
Quakers Coppice CW1: Crewe 3E 43
Quaker's Coppice Nature Reserve 3E 43
Quantock Cl. CW7: Wins 4C 22
Quantum Marshfield Bank Pk.
  CW2: Crewe 1D 40
Quarry Bank Ri. CW7: Wins 3D 22
Queen's Cres. CW1: Brad G 1E 35
Queen's Dr. CW5: Nant 2F 45
  CW10: Midd 4B 26
  CW11: Sandb 1C 32
Queensgate CW8: Nort 6G 9
Queens Pde. CW7: Wins 2F 23
Queens Pk. Dr. CW2: Crewe 1F 41
Queens Pk. Gdns. CW2: Crewe 1E 41
Queen St. CW1: Crewe 1C 42
  CW2: Shav 3A 48
  CW5: Nant 2G 45
  (off Hospital St.)
  CW9: Nort 5H 9
  CW10: Midd 2A 26
Queensway CW1: Crewe 1A 42
  CW7: Wins 3F 23

R

Racquets Ct., The CW10: Bost 4D 20
Radbroke Cl. CW11: Sandb 1F 33
Radcliffe Rd. CW7: Wins 5D 22
  CW11: Sandb 6B 32
Radnor Cl. CW11: Sandb 2A 32
Railbrook Ct. CW2: Crewe 3B 42
Rail Ho. CW2: Crewe 3B 42
Railton Av. CW1: Crewe 4G 35
Railway Age, The 2B 42
Railway St. CW2: Crewe 3B 42
Railway Vw. CW1: Crewe 1C 42
Rainbow St. CW1: Crewe 1B 42
Rainow Cl. CW10: Midd 4H 25
Ramsbottom St. CW1: Crewe 6H 35
  (not continuous)
Randle Bennett Cl. CW11: Elw 2A 32
Randle St. CW11: Sandb 1C 32
Ravendale Cl. CW7: Wins 2G 23
Ravens Cnr. CW5: Rave 5A 44
Ravenscroft CW4: Holm C 3C 28
Ravenscroft Cl. CW11: Sandb 2E 33
Ravenscroft Rd. CW2: Crewe 2E 41
Ravensfield CW8: Cudd 3B 12
Ravens La. CW5: Act, Burl, Rave 3A 44

RAVENSMOOR 5A 44
Ravenswood CW8: Hart 3D 14
Ray Av. CW5: Nant 6H 39
Rayleigh Av. CW9: Dave 1A 20
Rays Brow CW8: Barn 3D 8
Readesdale Av. CW2: Crewe 3F 41
REASEHEATH 3E 39
Rectory Cl. CW2: Wist 5E 41
  CW5: Nant 2G 45
Redbourne Dr. CW2: West 6H 49
Red Cow Ct. CW10: Midd 2A 26
  (off Wheelock St.)
Redesmere Cl. CW9: Nort 2A 16
  CW11: Sandb 2B 32
Redgate CW8: Nort 6F 9
Red La. CW11: Most 3G 31
Red Lion La. CW5: Nant 2F 45
Redshank Av. CW7: Wins 6E 23
Redshaw Cl. CW10: Midd 5A 26
Redstone Dr. CW7: Wins 2C 22
Redwood Cl. CW8: Barn 1D 8
Redwood Dr. CW1: Crewe 5F 35
Reed Bed (Nature Reserve) 5F 3
Reedsmere Wlk. CW9: Comb 3F 3
Rees Cres. CW4: Holm C 2E 29
Regal Cinema
  Northwich 5H 9
Regal Cl. CW9: Nort 3G 15
Regency Ct. CW7: Wins 4E 23
  (off Blenheim Dr.)
  CW10: Midd 3B 26
Regency Wlk. CW10: Midd 1B 26
Regency Way CW9: Nort 3G 15
Regent Cl. CW2: Shav 4H 47
Regents Ga. CW5: Nant 2A 46
Regent St. CW9: Moul 1H 19
Regents Way CW7: Wins 3C 22
  (off Newbury Av.)
  CW8: Cudd 3B 12
  (off Threeways)
Registry Cl. CW9: Nort 3G 15
Reid St. CW1: Crewe 5A 36
Remer St. CW1: Crewe 4B 36
Renaissance Ct. CW1: Crewe 2E 43
Renaissance Way CW1: Crewe 1E 43
Renshaw St. CW9: Nort 3D 10
Repton Dr. CW1: Hasl 6H 37
Retreat, The CW1: Crewe 5A 36
Reynolds La. CW11: Blet, Sandb 3G 33
  CW11: Sandb 2G 33
Rhoden St. CW1: Crewe 5E 37
Rhodes Cl. CW1: Hasl 1H 43
Ribble Av. CW7: Wins 2B 24
Ribble Pl. CW7: Wins 2B 24
Richard Moon St. CW1: Crewe 1H 41
Richardson Cl. CW2: Shav 2B 48
  CW11: Elw 3H 31
Richard St. CW1: Crewe 1H 41
  CW9: Nort 6C 10
Richmond Cl. CW2: West 6H 49
  CW11: Elw 2A 32
Richmond Ct. CW8: Hart 2E 15
Richmond Dr. CW9: Nort 3A 16
Richmond Rd. CW1: Crewe 1C 42
Richmond Village CW5: Nant 2A 46
Riddings Ct. CW8: Hart 3D 14
Riddings La. CW5: Wyb 6G 47
Ridgway St. CW1: Crewe 6B 36
Ridley Cl. CW2: Hou 5C 48
Rigby Av. CW1: Crewe 4G 35
Rigby's Row CW5: Nant 2G 45
Rigg St. CW1: Crewe 6H 35
Riley Cl. CW11: Etti H 4A 32
Rileys La. WA16: Pick 4F 5
Rilshaw La. CW7: Wins 3H 23
Rimsdale Cl. CW2: Wist 6G 41
Ripon Dr. CW2: Wist 5G 41
Riverbank Cl. CW5: Nant 5G 39
Riverside CW5: Nant 2F 45
  CW9: Nort 2B 16
Riverside Cres. CW4: Holm C 2E 29
Riverside Gro. CW2: Crewe 2D 40
Riverside Pk. CW8: Nort 1G 15
Riverside Trad. Est. CW8: Nort 6H 9
River Vw. CW7: Wins 2G 23
Road Beta CW10: Midd 3B 26

Road Five CW7: Wins 1C 24
Road Four CW7: Wins 1B 24
Road One CW1: Crewe 5H 43
   CW7: Wins 5B 20
Road One Rdbt. CW10: Wins 4B 20
Road Three CW7: Wins 2C 24
Road Two CW1: Crewe 5G 43
   CW7: Wins 1B 24
Roberts Dr. CW9: Rudh 1D 16
Roberts Rd. CW9: L Gral 3G 11
Robert St. CW8: Nort 1G 15
Robin Cl. CW11: Sandb 1C 32
Rochester Cres. CW1: Crewe 5D 36
Rockwood Av. CW2: Crewe 2G 41
Rockwood Cl. CW2: Crewe 2G 41
Roebuck St. CW1: Crewe 6A 36
Roedean Wlk. CW1: Crewe 5B 36
Roehurst La. CW7: Wins 1F 23
Roehurst Way CW7: Wins 1F 23
Rolls Av. CW1: Crewe 4F 35
Rolt Cres. CW10: Midd 3H 25
Romanes St. CW8: Nort 6G 9
Roman Way CW11: Sandb 2A 32
Rookery Cl. CW5: Nant 2H 45
   CW11: Etti H 4G 31
Rookery Ct. CW11: Etti H 4G 31
Rookery Dr. CW5: Nant 3G 45
Rookery Gdns. CW9: Dave 4G 15
Rookery Ri. CW7: Wins 3A 24
Rook St. CW2: Crewe 3A 42
Rope Bank Av. CW2: Wist 6G 41
Rope La. CW2: Shav, Wist 6F 41
Rosebank Cl. CW7: Wins 3H 23
Rosebank Wlk. CW8: Barn 1C 8
Roseberry Way CW1: Hasl 1G 43
Rose Farm Ct. CW9: Winc 1E 11
Rosehill Rd. CW2: Crewe 4H 41
Rosemount CW10: Midd 2A 26
   (off Lewin St.)
Rose Ter. CW1: Crewe 6A 36
Rose Tree Mdw. CW9: L Gral 3G 11
Rosewood Cl. CW1: Crewe 5C 36
Rosewood Dr. CW7: Wins 2C 22
Rossett Cl. CW9: Nort 3G 15
Rosslyn La. CW8: Cudd 4E 13
Rostherne Way CW11: Sandb 2B 32
Rowan Cl. CW7: Wins 6F 19
   CW10: Midd 5C 26
   CW11: Sandb 2B 32
Rowan Ri. CW8: Barn 2C 8
Rowan Rd. CW8: Weav 5H 7
Rowans, The CW9: Nort 1G 15
Rowans Cl. CW1: Crewe 4F 35
Rowton Cl. CW9: Nort 3H 15
Rowton Rd. CW2: Crewe 1D 40
Royal Arc. CW1: Crewe 1A 42
   (off Tower Way)
Royal Ct. CW9: Rudh 2D 16
Royal Gdns. CW9: Rudh 4G 15
Royal M. CW9: Rudh 2D 16
Royce Cl. CW1: Crewe 4G 35
Royds Cl. CW8: Hart 2D 14
Roylance Dr. CW10: Midd 3A 26
Royles Pl. CW8: Nort 1F 15
Royle St. CW7: Wins 2G 23
   CW9: Nort 5B 10
Rubin Dr. CW1: Crewe 4F 35
RUDHEATH .1D 16
Rudheath Cl. CW2: Crewe 6D 34
Rudheath Leisure Cen. 6D 10
Rudheath Way CW9: Rudh 2D 16
Rufford Cl. CW2: Wist 5H 41
RULOE 1A 12
Runcorn Rd. CW8: Barn, Lit L 6A 2
Ruscoe Av. CW11: Sandb 3A 32
Rushton Cl. CW9: Nort 6C 10
Rushton Dr. CW2: Hou 5C 48
   CW10: Midd 4A 26
Ruskin Rd. CW2: Crewe 2A 42
Russell Dr. CW1: Hasl 6G 37
Russell Rd. CW7: Wins 3E 23
Russet Cl. CW10: Midd 1H 25
Russet Rd. CW8: Weav 5H 7
Rutland Cl. CW11: Etti H 4G 31
Rutland Dr. CW8: Weav 4G 7
   CW10: Midd 4A 26
Ryburn Cl. CW2: West 4F 49

Rydal Cl. CW4: Holm C 4D 28
   CW7: Wins 6F 19
Rydal Mt. CW1: Leig 2H 35
Ryde Cl. CW1: Crewe 3H 35
Ryders St. CW8: Nort 5G 9
Ryebank Av. CW1: Wins 4H 35
Ryecroft Cl. CW10: Midd 4H 25

S

Sadler Cl. CW7: Wins 2F 23
Sadler Rd. CW7: Wins 2F 23
Sadler's Cl. CW4: Holm C 3D 28
St Albans Dr. CW5: Nant 4H 45
St Andrew's Av. CW2: Crewe 4A 42
St Andrews Cl. CW9: Rudh 6E 11
St Andrew's Ct. CW2: Crewe 4A 42
   (off St Andrew's Av.)
St Andrews Dr. CW4: Holm C 4D 28
St Annes Av. CW10: Midd 3A 26
St Anne's La. CW5: Nant 2F 45
St Ann's Rd. CW10: Midd 2H 25
St Ann's Wlk. CW10: Midd 2A 26
   (off Beech St.)
St Augustine's Dr. CW2: Eng B 3H 48
   (off Abbey Pk. Way)
St Bede's Av. CW8: Weav 4H 7
St Catherine Dr. CW8: Hart 3B 14
St Chads Cl. CW5: Wyb 6G 47
St Chad's Flds. CW7: Wins 6E 23
St Clair St. CW2: Crewe 4B 42
St Clements Cl. CW2: West 6F 49
St Georges Ct. CW2: Eng B 4H 49
   (off Abbey Pk. Way)
St George's Rd. CW7: Wins 3E 23
St George's Way CW9: Nort 2H 15
St Helens Rd. CW9: Nort 5A 10
St James Ter. CW7: Wins 3C 22
   (off Cavendish Cl.)
St James Wlk. CW8: Nort 6G 9
   (off Beeston St.)
St James Way CW8: Hart 2E 15
St John's Av. CW9: L Gral 2F 11
St John's Cl. CW9: Rudh 6E 11
St Johns Ct. CW7: Wins 2D 22
St Johns Dr. CW7: Wins 3C 22
St John's Way CW8: Sandi 5E 13
   CW11: Sandb 3G 33
St Josephs Way CW5: Nant 2A 46
St Lawrence Ct. CW5: Nant 1H 45
St Lukes Cl. CW4: Holm C 3F 29
St Mary's Av. CW8: Weav 4H 7
St Marys Ct. CW5: Act 6C 38
St Mary's Dr. CW8: Whit 1B 18
St Mary's Rd. CW5: Nant 6G 39
St Mary's St. CW1: Crewe 1A 42
St Matthews Cl. CW1: Hasl 1H 43
St Michael's Cl. CW8: Lit L 1H 7
St Michael's Vw. CW1: Crewe 6H 35
   (off Rigg St.)
St Michael's Way CW10: Midd 2A 26
St Paul's Cl. CW1: Crewe 1A 42
St Pauls Pl. CW9: Nort 4A 10
   (off Witton St.)
St Paul's St. CW1: Crewe 1A 42
   (not continuous)
St Peter's Ri. CW11: Sandb 2A 32
St Stephens Ct. CW11: Elw 2H 31
St Vincent Dr. CW8: Hart 3B 14
St Wilfrid's Ct. CW9: Dave 4A 16
Salander Cres. CW2: Wist 6G 41
Salisbury Av. CW2: Crewe 4A 42
Salisbury Cl. CW2: Crewe 4H 41
Salkeld St. CW1: Crewe 5B 10
Salters Ford CW8: Barn 2B 8
SALTERSWALL 6B 18
Salt Line Way CW11: Elw 3H 31
Saltmeadows CW5: Nant 2E 45
Salt Mus., The 6H 9
Samian Cl. CW10: Midd 1A 26
Samuel St. CW1: Crewe 6H 35
Sanhec Way CW11: Sandb 3D 32
   (off Penda Way)
SANDBACH .3D 32
Sandbach Crosses 3D 32
   (off Market Sq.)

Sandbach Dr. CW9: Nort 1G 15
SANDBACH HEATH 3F 33
Sandbach Leisure Cen. 2C 32
SANDBACH SERVICE AREA 4H 33
Sandbach Station (Rail) 2H 31
Sanderson Cl. CW2: Crewe 5A 42
   (off Davenport Av.)
Sanderson Way CW10: Midd 2C 26
Sandfield La. CW8: Act B 4C 6
   CW8: Hart 3E 15
Sandford Cres. CW2: West 5H 49
Sandford Rd. CW5: Nant 6H 39
Sandhole La. CW8: Crow 6A 6
Sandhurst Av. CW2: Crewe 4G 41
Sandiford Rd. CW4: Holm C 3E 29
Sandiford Sq. CW9: Nort 5A 10
Sandington Dr. CW8: Sandi 5D 12
SANDIWAY .4E 13
Sandiway Cl. CW8: Sandi 5E 13
Sandiway La. CW9: Antr 2C 2
Sandiway Pk. CW8: Hart 3A 14
Sandiway Rd. CW7: Wins 5G 35
Sandon Pk. Gdns. CW2: Crewe 1D 40
Sandon St. CW1: Crewe 1B 42
Sandown Cl. CW10: Midd 3A 26
Sandown Cres. CW8: Cudd 4E 13
Sandown Rd. CW1: Crewe 4A 36
Sandringham Cl. CW7: Wins 6E 19
   CW9: Nort 3G 15
Sandringham Ct. CW4: Holm C 3E 29
Sandringham Dr. CW2: Wist 6E 41
Sandringham Pl. CW8: Hart 2E 15
Sandybank CW8: Winn 4F 9
Sandyhill Pl. CW7: Wins 5F 23
Sandyhill Rd. CW7: Wins 5E 23
Sandylands Pk. CW2: Wist 6D 40
Sandy La. CW8: Weav 2F 7
   CW8: Whit 3A 18
   CW11: Etti H 4H 31
Sandymere Ct. CW7: Wins 2D 22
Sandy Way CW7: Wins 3D 22
Saughall Cl. CW1: Crewe 3G 15
Saunders St. CW1: Crewe 1H 41
Saunton Cl. CW7: Wins 1C 22
Saville Ri. CW7: Wins 2G 23
Savoy Rd. CW1: Crewe 5E 43
Saxon Crossway CW7: Wins 2H 22
Saxons La. CW8: Nort 6F 9
   (off Heysoms La.)
   CW8: Nort 1G 15
   (Alfred St.)
Saxon Way CW11: Sandb 3E 33
   (off Palmer Rd.)
Scaife Rd. CW5: Nant 1H 45
School Cres. CW1: Crewe 1C 42
School Dr. CW8: Barn 2C 8
SCHOOL GREEN 6E 23
School La. CW5: Nant 1G 45
   CW8: Hart 2D 14
   CW8: Sandi 5E 13
   CW9: Gt B 3B 4
   CW9: L Gral 3G 11
   CW9: Moul 1G 19
   CW11: Elw 2H 31
   CW11: Sandb 3G 33
   CW11: Warm 2B 30
   WA16: Pick 1H 5
School Rd. CW7: Mead 4F 19
   CW7: Wins 1A 24
   CW9: Rudh 2D 16
School Rd. Nth. CW9: Rudh 1E 17
   (not continuous)
School Rd. Sth. CW9: Rudh 1D 16
School St. CW1: Hasl 6H 37
School Way CW9: Nort 5A 10
Scotch Hall La. CW9: Antr 1B 2
Scott Av. CW1: Crewe 1D 42
Scott Cl. CW11: Elw 3H 31
Sea Bank CW10: Midd 2B 26
Seagrave Cl. CW9: Nort 2H 15
Seagull Cl. CW1: Crewe 6D 36
Seaton Cl. CW1: Crewe 3H 35
Seaton St. CW7: Wins 2D 24
Second Av. CW1: Crewe 4D 42
   CW11: Sandb 4C 32
Second Wood St. CW5: Nant 2F 45
Sedbergh Cl. CW4: Holm C 3C 28

Seddon St. CW10: Midd 1A 26
Sedgemere Av. CW1: Crewe 3G 35
Selkirk Dr. CW4: Holm C 4D 28
Selsey Cl. CW1: Crewe 3H 35
Selworthy Dr. CW1: Crewe 4H 35
Senna La. CW9: Antr, Comb 2C 2
Severn Wlk. CW7: Wins 1A 24
Shady Brook La. CW8: Weav 4G 7
Shakespeare Cl. CW9: Nort 6C 10
Shakespeare Dr. CW1: Crewe 1E 43
Shannon Cl. CW5: Will 2D 46
Sharnbrook Dr. CW2: Crewe 1E 41
SHAVINGTON 3H 47
Shavington Leisure Cen. 2G 47
Shavington Way CW9: Nort 3G 15
Shaws La. CW7: Wins 5H 19
Sheath St. CW9: Nort 5A 10
Shelburne Dr. CW1: Hasl 6G 37
Shelley Av. CW9: Winc 6F 5
Shelley Cl. CW1: Crewe 1D 42
CW10: Midd 6C 26
Shelley Ct. CW11: Etti H 3H 31
Shelley Dr. CW2: Wist 4F 41
Shepherds Fold Dr. CW7: Wins 6E 19
Sheppard Cl. CW1: Crewe 6B 36
Sherborne Rd. CW1: Crewe 5B 36
Sherbourne Ct. CW2: Eng B 4H 49
(off Golden Hill)
Sheridan Cl. CW1: Leig 2H 35
Sheringham Dr. CW1: Crewe 3H 35
Sherratt Cl. CW5: Nant 3H 45
Sherwin St. CW2: Crewe 3A 42
Shilton Cl. CW10: Midd 5C 26
Shipbrook Rd. CW9: Dave, What 4A 16
CW9: Nort, Rudh 2C 16
Shores Grn. Dr. CW9: Winc 6F 5
Shorthorn Cl. CW10: Midd 1B 26
Shrewbridge Cres. CW5: Nant 3G 45
Shrewbridge Rd. CW5: B'ton, Nant 5F 45
Shropshire Cl. CW10: Midd 3H 25
Shurlach Rd. CW9: Rudh 2C 16
Shutley La. CW8: Lit L 1H 7
Siddall St. CW9: Nort 5B 10
Siddals Ct. CW5: Nant 2E 45
(off Welsh Row)
Siddington Av. CW9: Nort 3A 16
Siddorn St. CW7: Wins 2G 23
Silverdale CW8: Winn 6F 9
Silverdale Cl. CW2: West 5G 49
Silver Ter. CW11: Sandb 3F 33
Simmonds Cl. CW9: Nort 4G 15
Simonswood Cl. CW10: Midd 3H 25
Simpson Ct. CW1: Leig 2H 35
Singleton Av. CW1: Crewe 5A 36
Sir John Deane's Leisure Cen. 1H 15
Skeath Cl. CW11: Sandb 3G 33
Skylark Cl. CW1: Crewe 4F 35
Slade St. CW9: Nort 5B 10
Slaughter Hill CW1: Crewe G, Hasl 2H 43
Slicks Bus. Cen. CW8: Winn 3E 9
Smallbrook Wlk. CW2: Crewe 5A 42
(off Davenport Av.)
Smallman Rd. CW2: Crewe 4H 41
Smallwood Cl. CW10: Midd 3A 26
Smithers Cl. CW5: Nant 3H 45
Smithfield Cl. CW11: Sandb 3E 33
Smith Gro. CW1: Crewe 5F 35
Smith's La. CW8: Weav 4G 7
Smithy Bank CW5: Act 1C 44
Smithy Fold CW8: Barn 3D 8
(off Lydyett La.)
Smithy La. CW1: Crewe, Leig 3E 35
CW2: West 2G 49
CW8: Cudd, Gors 2E 13
CW9: Gt B 3A 4
CW9: L Gral 3G 11
Smithy Wlk. CW11: Sandb 6B 32
Smokehall La. CW7: Moul, Wins 3G 19
Smokehall La. Ind. Est.
CW7: Wins 4A 20
Snape La. CW2: Eng B, West 3H 49
Snape Rd. CW2: Crewe 5B 42
Snowdon Dr. CW2: Crewe 2D 40
Snowdonia Way CW7: Wins 3D 22
Snowdon St. CW8: Barn 2B 8
Solvay Rd. CW8: Winn 3F 9
(not continuous)

Somerford Av. CW2: Crewe 2G 41
Somerford Cl. CW11: Sandb 1E 33
Somerley Cl. CW1: Crewe 3H 35
Somerville St. CW2: Crewe 3H 41
Soot Hill CW9: And, Barn 2E 9
Sorbus Dr. CW1: Crewe 5C 36
South La. CW5: Rave, Soun 5A 44
South Av. CW1: Hasl 1H 43
Southbank CW9: Gt B 4A 4
Southbank Av. CW2: Shav 2A 48
SOUTH CHESHIRE PRIVATE HOSPITAL . . .2E 35
South Crofts CW5: Nant 2G 45
South Dr. CW9: Rudh 1D 16
Southey Cl. CW11: Etti H 4H 31
Southlands CW4: Holm C 4E 29
Southmere Ct. CW1: Crewe 3E 43
South St. CW2: Crewe 3B 42
Southwark Pl. CW7: Wins 3C 22
Southway CW10: Midd 2A 26
(off St Ann's Rd.)
Sovereign Cl. CW9: Rudh 1F 17
Spencer Cl. CW2: Wist 5G 41
Spencer St. CW8: Barn 2D 8
CW8: Nort 6G 9
Spey Cl. CW7: Wins 1H 23
CW10: Midd 1B 26
Spink La. WA16: Pick 5G 5
Spinner Cres. CW9: Comb 4F 3
Spinney, The CW5: Will 1D 46
CW8: Cudd 2B 12
CW11: Sandb 3E 33
Spinney Cl. CW7: Wins 3A 24
Spinney Dr. CW2: West 2F 49
Springbank Cres. CW7: Wins 3E 23
Spring Farm Bus. Cen.
CW1: Mins V 1G 35
Springfield Cres. CW8: Barn 2B 8
Springfield Dr. CW2: Wist 6F 41
Springfields CW8: Cudd 3B 12
Spring Gdns. CW1: Crewe 6C 36
CW5: Nant 2H 45
Spring Mdw. CW8: Winn 4G 9
Springvale Bus. Cen.
CW11: Etti H 3H 31
Springvale Ct. CW11: Etti H 3H 31
Springvale Ind. Est. CW11: Etti H 3H 31
Springwater Dr. CW2: Nant 5G 49
Springwell Cl. CW2: Wist 5A 42
SPROSTON GREEN 1G 27
Sproston Way CW9: Nort 3G 15
Spruce Av. CW8: Sandi 4F 13
Square, The CW4: Holm C 3E 29
Squirrel Cl. CW8: Nort 6E 9
Stable M. CW8: Sandi 6E 13
Stables, The CW10: Bost 4D 20
Stafford St. CW1: Crewe 6A 36
Stalbridge Rd. CW2: Crewe 3A 42
Stallard Way CW10: Midd 3A 26
Stamford Av. CW2: Crewe 2A 42
Stamp Av. CW1: Crewe 5B 36
Stamp Cl. CW1: Crewe 5B 36
Standford Dr. CW9: Nort 2A 16
Stanford St. CW9: Nort 2H 15
Stanhope Av. CW1: Crewe 2C 42
Stanier Cl. CW1: Crewe 1E 43
Stanley Cl. CW8: Hart 3C 14
Stanley Gro. CW9: Nort 3E 11
Stanley St. CW1: Crewe 1A 42
CW9: Nort 5C 10
Stannerhouse La. CW11: Blet, Malk B 6F 33
Stanthorne Av. CW2: Crewe 2F 41
Stanthorne Pk. M. CW10: Stan 5E 25
Stanyer Ct. CW5: Stap 3A 46
Stapeley Cl. CW9: Nort 3G 15
Stapeley Ct. CW1: Crewe 6H 35
Stapeley Grange Wildlife Hospital 6B 46
Stapeley Ter. CW5: Nant 3A 46
Stapeley Water Gardens 4A 46
Station Hill CW8: Act B 4D 6
Station Rd. CW4: Holm C 4E 29
CW5: Nant 2G 45
CW7: Wins 2H 23
CW8: Act B, Weav 3D 6
CW8: Crow 3A 6
CW9: L Gral 3G 11
CW9: Nort 4B 10
CW11: Elw 2H 31

Station Vw. CW5: Nant 3G 45
CW11: Elw 1H 31
Station Yd. Trad. Est. CW4: Holm C 3F 29
(off Station Rd.)
Staveley Dr. CW7: Wins 1F 23
Steele Rd. CW10: Midd 6B 26
Stephenson Dr. CW1: Crewe 1E 43
Stephenson Wlk. CW7: Wins 3C 22
Sterne Cl. CW11: Elw 3H 31
Stewart St. CW2: Crewe 2G 41
Stiles, The CW8: Cudd 2C 12
Stirling Cl. CW7: Wins 1A 24
CW9: Nort 2H 15
Stirling Ct. CW4: Holm C 4D 28
Stock La. CW2: Shav 6G 47
CW5: Shav, Wyb 6G 47
Stocks Hill CW7: Wins 4G 23
Stonebridge Rd. CW5: Nant 4G 45
Stonecroft CW9: Nort 2A 16
Stoneheyes La. CW8: Barn 1B 8
CW9: Barn 1B 8
Stoneley Av. CW1: Crewe 4A 36
STONELEY GREEN 3A 44
Stoneley Rd. CW1: Crewe 4B 36
Stones Mnr. La. CW8: Hart 2E 15
STONEYFORD 4A 12
Stoneyford La. CW8: Cudd, Oak 4A 12
STOWFORD .6G 43
Strathaven Av. CW2: Wist 5E 41
Strathmore Cl. CW4: Holm C 4D 28
Strawberry La. CW8: Act B 2D 6
Stretton Wlk. CW9: Nort 3H 15
Stringer Av. CW11: Sandb 4E 33
Stuart Cl. CW7: Wins 6E 23
Stubbs La. CW9: L Gral 3G 11
Styal Cl. CW9: Nort 3H 15
Summer Dr. CW1: Sandb 3E 33
Summerfield Dr. CW9: Moul 1H 19
Sunart Cl. CW2: Wist 1H 47
Sundale Dr. CW2: Crewe 2D 40
Sunningdale Cl. CW7: Wins 1C 22
CW9: Rudh 6E 11
Sunnybank Rd. CW1: Crewe, Wool 6E 35
CW2: Crewe, Wool 6E 35
Sunnymill Dr. CW11: Sandb 3C 32
Surrey St. CW1: Crewe 1C 42
Sutton Cl. CW5: Nant 2E 45
CW9: Winc 5F 5
Sutton Fld. CW8: Whit 2C 18
Sutton La. CW10: Midd 6H 25
Swallow Cl. CW7: Wins 6F 23
Swallow Dr. CW11: Sandb 1C 32
Swallowfield Cl. CW2: Wist 5G 41
Swanage Ct. CW7: Wins 6F 23
Swan Cl. CW8: Crow 6C 6
SWANLEY 1A 44
Swanley La. CW5: Act, B'ley, Burl, Rave . . .1A 44
Swanlow Av. CW7: Wins 6F 23
Swanlow Dr. CW7: Wins 6E 23
Swanlow La. CW7: Wins 3E 23
Swanscoe Cl. CW10: Midd 3H 25
Sweet Briar Cl. CW8: Barn 1D 8
Sweet Briar Cres. CW2: Crewe 2F 41
Sweettooth Cl. CW11: Sandb 2C 32
Swettenham Cl. CW11: Sandb 2F 33
Swift Cl. CW2: Wist 5F 41
Swinburne Dr. CW1: Crewe 1D 42
Swine Mkt. CW5: Nant 2G 45
Swinnerton St. CW2: Crewe 3A 42
Sycamore Av. CW1: Crewe 5B 36
CW7: Wins 3E 23
Sycamore Cl. CW4: Holm C 3E 29
CW5: Nant 6H 39
Sycamore Cres. CW8: Barn 1D 8
Sycamore Dr. CW10: Midd 6B 26
Sycamore Gro. CW11: Sandb 1C 32
SYDNEY 6E 37
Sydney Rd. CW1: Crewe 4C 36
Sydney St. CW8: Nort 6E 9
Sylvan Cl. CW8: Nort 1E 15

T

Tabley Cl. CW11: Sandb 2A 32
Tabley Rd. CW2: Crewe 2E 41
Tabley St. CW9: Nort 4A 10

Tailors Vw. *CW5: Nant* 1G **45**
   (off Arnold St.)
Talbot Cl. CW2: Shav 3H **47**
Talbot Way CW5: Stap 4H **45**
Tall Trees Cl. CW8: Nort 1E **15**
Tamar Wlk. CW7: Wins 6A **20**
Tame Cl. CW11: Sandb 1A **32**
Tanners Way CW5: Nant 3G **45**
Tarn Cl. CW7: Wins 1E **23**
Tarporley Rd. CW8: Oak, Sandi 6C **12**
Tarvin Av. CW2: Crewe 1D **40**
Tarvin Cl. CW9: Nort 2H **15**
  CW10: Midd 6B **26**
Tarvin Way CW7: Wins 1E **23**
Tate Dr. CW1: Hasl 1G **43**
Tatton Cl. CW7: Wins 2D **22**
  CW9: Nort 3H **15**
Tatton Dr. CW11: Sandb 2E **33**
Tatton Rd. CW2: Crewe 3E **41**
Taxmere Cl. CW11: Sandb 2B **32**
Taylor Dr. CW5: Nant 2E **45**
Tealby Cl. CW9: Nort 5B **10**
Teal Cl. CW7: Wins 6F **23**
Telfer Ct. CW10: Midd 5C **26**
Telford Gdns. CW11: Sandb 6B **32**
Telford Pl. CW5: Nant 2E **45**
Telford Way CW10: Midd 2C **26**
Tenchersfield CW5: Nant 3A **46**
Tennyson Av. CW1: Crewe 1D **42**
Tennyson Cl. CW2: Wist 4G **41**
  CW9: Nort 1C **16**
Tewkesbury Cl. CW10: Midd 2H **25**
Thackery Ct. CW11: Etti H 3H **31**
Thames Pl. *CW7: Wins* 2B **24**
   (off Trent Av.)
The . . . .
  Names prefixed with 'The' for example
  'The Aspens' are indexed under the main
  name such as 'Aspens, The'
Theatre Ct. CW9: Nort 5H **9**
Third Av. CW1: Crewe 4D **42**
  CW11: Sandb .4C **32**
Thirlmere Cl. CW4: Holm C 3C **28**
  CW7: Wins 6H **19**
Thirlmere Rd. CW2: Crewe 4F **41**
Thistle Cl. WA16: Pick 4F **5**
Thomas Av. CW5: Stap 4A **46**
Thomas Hodges Ct. CW4: Holm C 3F **29**
Thomas Row *CW5: Nant* 1G **45**
   (off Dog La.)
Thomas St. CW1: Crewe 6B **36**
Thorley Gro. CW2: Crewe 4G **41**
Thornbrook Way CW11: Etti H 4H **31**
Thornfields CW1: Leig 2H **35**
Thorn La. CW8: Hart 2E **15**
Thornton Cl. CW7: Wins 6A **20**
Thornton Dr. CW2: Wist 6G **41**
Thorn Tree Dr. CW1: Leig 2G **35**
Thornycroft CW7: Wins 2C **22**
Thorpe Cl. CW1: Crewe 3F **35**
Threeways CW8: Cudd 3B **12**
Thrush Way CW7: Wins 5H **19**
Tiffield St. CW7: Wins 5A **20**
Tilstone Cl. CW2: Hou 5C **48**
  CW9: Nort 2A **16**
Timber La. CW9: Nort 4H **9**
Timbrell Av. CW1: Crewe 5F **35**
Tinkersfield CW5: Stap 3A **46**
Tiverton Cl. CW11: Sandb 2E **33**
Tiverton Ct. *CW9: Nort* 2G **15**
   (off Blakemere Dr.)
Tollemache Dr. CW1: Crewe 3G **35**
Tollitt St. CW1: Crewe 1A **42**
Tomkinson Cl. CW1: Crewe 4F **35**
Tommy's La. CW1: Crewe 3C **42**
Tourist Info. Cen.
  Nantwich 2G **45**
Tower La. CW8: Weav 4F **7**
Towers Cl. CW2: Wist 6G **41**
Tower Way CW1: Crewe 1A **42**
Townbridge Ct. CW8: Nort 5H **9**
Townfield Ct. CW8: Barn 2D **8**
Townfield La. CW8: Barn 1C **8**
TOWN FIELDS 4E **23**
Town Flds. CW11: Sandb 4C **32**
Townfields Cotts. *CW7: Wins* 4F **23**
   (off Swanlow La.)

Townfields Cres. CW7: Wins 4F **23**
Townfields Dr. CW7: Wins 5E **23**
Townfields Gdns. CW7: Wins 4F **23**
Townfields Rd. CW7: Wins 4F **23**
Townshend Rd. CW9: L Gral 2G **11**
Town Sq. CW9: Nort 5H **9**
Trackside Bus. Pk.
  CW11: Etti H 3G **31**
Trafalgar Cl. CW9: Nort 4G **15**
Trent Av. CW7: Wins 2B **24**
Trent Cl. CW7: Wins 2B **24**
Trevithick Cl. CW1: Crewe 1E **43**
Trickett La. CW8: Cudd 4E **13**
Tricketts La. CW5: Will 2E **47**
Tricketts M. CW5: Will 2E **47**
Trinity Cl. CW2: Crewe 4G **41**
Trinity Ter. *CW8: Nort* 6G **9**
   (off Waterloo St.)
Troon Cl. CW4: Holm C 4E **29**
Troutbeck Gro. CW7: Wins 1F **23**
Tudor Cl. CW7: Wins 5F **23**
  CW9: Rudh 1E **17**
  CW10: Midd 2B **26**
   (off Regency Ct.)
Tudor Way CW5: Nant 4G **45**
Tunbridge Cl. CW2: Wist 5G **41**
Tunnel Rd. CW8: Barn 3D **8**
Tunnel Top CW8: Barn 3C **8**
Turnberry Cl. CW7: Wins 1E **23**
  CW9: Rudh 6E **11**
Turner Cl. CW1: Crewe 3G **35**
Turner St. CW5: Nant 2H **45**
Turnpike Cl. CW11: Sandb 2A **32**
Twemlow Av. CW11: Sandb 1D **32**
TWEMLOW GREEN 1H **29**
Twemlow Grn. CW4: Holm C 1H **29**
Tyldesley Way CW5: Nant 1F **45**
Tynedale Av. CW2: Crewe 3H **41**
Tytherington Cl. CW10: Midd 5A **26**

U

Ullswater Av. CW2: Crewe 2E **41**
  CW7: Wins 1E **23**
Underwood Cl. CW1: Crewe 5H **35**
Underwood Ind. Pk.
  CW1: Crewe 5G **35**
Underwood La. CW1: Crewe 6H **35**
Union St. CW2: Crewe 2B **42**
  CW11: Sandb .3D **32**
University Way CW1: Crewe 2E **43**
Uplands CW8: Cudd 3B **12**
Uplands Rd. CW9: And 1F **9**
Up. Haigh St. CW7: Wins 3E **23**
Upton Cl. CW7: Wins 5H **19**
Ursuline Way CW2: Crewe 4H **41**

V

Valebrook Dr. CW5: Wyb 6G **47**
Vale Rd. CW8: Hart .3E **15**
  CW9: Mars 5B **4**
Vale Royal Dr. CW8: Whit 2C **18**
Vale Vw. CW9: Nort 4D **10**
Valley Brook Bus. Cen.
  CW2: Crewe 2B **42**
   (off Lord St.)
Valley Ct. CW10: Midd 2C **26**
Valley La. CW8: Cudd 4D **12**
Valley Rd. CW2: Crewe 4F **41**
  CW8: Weav 4G **7**
Valley Vw. CW9: Nort 6C **10**
Vauxhall Pl. CW5: Nant 6G **39**
Vauxhall Rd. CW5: Nant 6G **39**
Vauxhall Way CW7: Wins 5E **23**
Vearow's Pl. *CW9: Nort* 6H **9**
   (off Queen St.)
Venables Rd. CW9: Nort 5A **10**
Venables Way CW10: Midd 5C **26**
Ventnor Cl. CW10: Midd 3A **26**
Verdin Av. CW9: Nort 4H **9**
Verdin Cl. CW7: Wins 1E **23**
  CW9: Moul 1H **19**
Verdin Ct. CW1: Crewe 3G **35**
Verdin Exchange CW7: Wins 2F **23**

Verdin St. CW9: Nort 5C **10**
Vere St. CW1: Crewe 6A **36**
Verity Cl. CW1: Hasl 1G **43**
Verity Ct. CW10: Midd 1C **26**
Vernon St. CW1: Crewe 6H **35**
Vernon Way CW1: Crewe 6B **36**
Vicarage Gdns. CW11: Elw 1A **32**
Vicarage Gro. CW7: Wins 6F **23**
Vicarage La. CW11: Blet 5F **33**
  CW11: Elw 2A **32**
Vicarage Rd. CW1: Hasl 5H **37**
  CW9: Nort 5B **10**
Vicarage Wlk. CW9: Nort 6B **10**
Vickers Way CW9: Nort 6A **10**
Victoria Av. CW1: Hasl 1G **43**
  CW2: Crewe 1E **41**
  CW4: Holm C 4E **29**
Victoria Cen. CW1: Crewe 1A **42**
Victoria Gallery 2G **45**
   (off Market St.)
VICTORIA INFIRMARY 5G **9**
Victoria Mill Dr. CW5: Will 1D **46**
Victoria Pk. CW8: Nort 4H **9**
Victoria Rd. CW9: Nort 5B **10**
Victoria Sq. CW7: Wins 3C **22**
Victoria Stadium 2D **10**
Victoria St. CW1: Crewe 1A **42**
  CW9: Nort 3E **11**
  CW11: Sandb .2C **32**
Village Cl. CW9: L Gre 5G **11**
Village Farm CW5: Act 6C **38**
Villiers Russell Cl.
  CW1: Crewe 6B **36**
Vincent St. CW1: Crewe 1C **42**
Vine Tree Av. CW2: Crewe 3H **41**
  CW2: Shav 2H **47**
Vineyard, The CW2: Shav 2H **47**
Volunteer Av. CW5: Nant 1G **45**
Volunteer Flds. CW5: Nant 1G **45**

W

Wadebrook Trad. Est. *CW9: Nort* 5C **10**
   (off Hargreaves Rd.)
Wade Cres. CW8: Barn 1C **8**
Wades La. CW7: Wins 6E **19**
Wade St. CW9: Nort 4B **10**
Waine St. CW1: Crewe 6B **36**
Wakefield Cl. CW7: Wins 4F **35**
Wakefield Ct. CW9: Nort 2A **16**
Walcroft Gdns. CW10: Midd 2A **26**
Waldron Gdns. CW2: Crewe 4F **41**
Waldron Rd. CW1: Hasl 2H **43**
Waldron's La. CW1: Crewe 2B **36**
Walford Av. CW2: Crewe 2H **41**
Walker Cl. CW1: Hasl 1H **43**
Walker Dr. CW10: Midd 3A **26**
Walker St. CW1: Crewe 6H **35**
Wallace Cl. CW7: Wins 2D **24**
Wallace St. CW8: Nort 6G **9**
Walled Garden, The
  CW10: Bost 4C **20**
Wallerscote Cl. CW8: Weav 5A **8**
Wallerscote Rd.
  CW8: Hart, Weav 5H **7**
Wallfields Cl. CW5: Nant 6G **39**
Wallfields Rd. CW5: Nant 6G **39**
Wall Hill Way CW8: Act B 2D **6**
Wallis St. CW1: Crewe 1B **42**
Wall La. CW5: Nant .1F **45**
Walmer Pl. CW7: Wins 5E **23**
Walnut Av. CW8: Weav 5G **7**
Walnut Dr. CW7: Wins 2A **24**
Walnut La. CW8: Hart 2C **14**
Walpole Cl. CW1: Hasl 6G **37**
Walthall St. CW2: Crewe 2A **42**
Warburton Cl. CW8: Barn 1B **8**
Warburton Way *CW11: Sandb* 3D **32**
   (off High La.)
Wardle M. CW10: Midd 3A **26**
Wareham Dr. CW1: Crewe 3H **35**
WARMINGHAM 2B **30**
Warmingham Ct. CW10: Midd 4B **26**
Warmingham La. CW10: Midd 4B **26**
  CW11: Most 1F **31**
WARMINGHAM MOSS 6A **30**

Warmingham Rd.
CW1: Crewe, Warm 2A 36
CW1: Warm 2B 30
CW11: Warm 2B 30
Warm Walls *CW11: Sandb* 3D 32
(off High St.)
Warren, The CW8: Cudd 2B 12
Warren Av. CW9: L Gral 2G 11
Warren Cl. CW10: Midd 4H 25
Warren La. CW8: Hart 3C 14
Warrington Av. CW1: Crewe 5A 36
Warrington Rd. CW8: Act B, Lit L 1E 7
CW8: Cudd 3D 12
CW9: Comb 4F 3
Warwick Pl. CW7: Wins 5E 23
Wasdale Gro. CW1: Leig 2H 35
Waste La. CW8: Cudd 4C 12
Watch La. CW11: Most 3E 31
(not continuous)
Watchlane Flash (Nature Reserve) 3F 31
Waterbank Row CW9: Nort 6H 9
Water-Lode CW5: Nant 1E 45
Waterloo Rd. CW1: Hasl 1H 43
CW8: Nort 6G 9
Waters Edge CW9: And 2F 9
Waters Edge M. CW10: Midd 3A 26
Waterside M. CW11: Sandb 6C 32
Waterside Vw. CW9: Rudh 6E 11
Waterside Way CW10: Midd 1H 25
Water St. CW9: Nort 6H 9
Watling Ct. CW8: Sandi 5F 13
Watling St. CW9: Nort 5H 9
Waverley Ct. CW2: Crewe 3B 42
Waverton Cl. CW2: Hou 5C 48
CW9: Nort 3G 15
Wavertree Dr. CW10: Midd 4H 25
Waybutt La. CW2: Balt, Chor 6F 49
Wayfarers Ct. WA16: Pick 4F 5
WAYS GREEN 3G 23
Way's Grn. CW7: Wins 3G 23
Waystead Cl. CW9: Nort 3H 15
Weaver Bank CW5: Nant 2F 45
Weaver Cl. CW11: Sandb 2A 32
Weaver Ct. *CW9: Nort* 5H 9
(off London Rd.)
Weaver Grange CW9: Moul 1G 19
Weaverhall La. CW7: Darn 6A 24
WEAVERHAM 5H 7
Weaverham Leisure & Community Cen. . . .5H 7
Weaverham Rd.
CW8: Cudd, Gors, Sandi 5E 13
Weaver Parkway Country Pk. 3F 19
Weaver Rd. CW5: Nant 1G 45
CW8: Nort 6G 9
CW9: Moul 2G 19
Weaverside CW5: Nant 5G 45
Weaver St. CW7: Wins 3G 23
Weaver Valley Rd. CW7: Wins 6H 19
Weaver Vw. CW8: Nort 6H 9
CW8: Weav 4H 7
Weaver Way CW9: Nort 5H 9
Webb's Ct. CW9: Nort 6H 9
Webb's La. CW10: Midd 1A 26
Weir St. CW9: Nort 6H 9
Welbeck Cl. CW10: Midd 2H 25
Welland Cl. CW11: Etti H 4G 31
Well Bank CW11: Sandb 3D 32
Wellcroft Cl. CW2: Wist 6H 41
Wellesley Av. CW1: Hasl 1G 43
Welles St. CW11: Sandb 2D 32
Wellfield CW7: Wins 1A 24
Wellfield Cl. WA16: Pick 4G 5
Wellington Rd. CW5: Nant 3G 45
Wellington St. CW8: Nort 6G 9
Well La. CW8: Weav 3G 7
Wells Av. CW1: Hasl 6H 37
WELLS GREEN 6G 41
Well St. CW7: Wins 2E 23
Wellwood Dr. CW2: Wist 6F 41
Welsh La. CW7: Wins 5F 23
Welshman's La.
CW5: Henh, Nant 6E 39
Welsh Row CW5: Nant 1E 45
Wentworth Cl. CW9: Rudh 6E 11
Wentworth Gro. CW7: Wins 6C 18
Wesley Av. CW11: Sandb 3D 32
Wesley Cl. CW5: Nant 2G 45

Wesley Ct. CW7: Wins 2H 23
Wesley Pl. CW2: Crewe 3B 42
CW9: Nort 5A 10
Wessex Cl. CW7: Wins 4A 48
Wessex Dr. CW9: Rudh 1C 16
Westage La.
CW9: Ast B, Budw H, Gt B 3A 4
West Av. CW1: Crewe 1H 41
CW2: West 2F 49
CW9: Rudh 1D 16
CW10: Midd 1A 26
Westbourne Av. CW1: Crewe 5G 35
Westbury Cl. CW2: Wist 5A 42
CW8: Nort 3A 26
West Dr. CW7: Wins 1A 24
W. Dudley St. CW7: Wins 2H 23
Western Av. CW5: Nant 4G 45
Westfield CW7: Wins 6E 23
Westfield Dr. CW2: Wist 5E 41
Westfield Gro. CW8: Barn 1B 8
Westfield Rd. CW9: Nort 6B 10
Westgate Av. CW7: Wins 2C 22
Westgate Pk. CW7: Hou 5C 48
Westholme Cl. CW2: Crewe 5A 42
Westlands Rd. CW10: Midd 2H 25
West La. CW8: Cudd 4D 12
Westmere Cl. CW2: West 2F 49
Westmere Dr. CW1: Crewe 3D 42
Westminster Cl. CW8: Hart 2E 15
CW10: Midd 2H 25
Westminster Gro. *CW7: Wins* 3C 22
(off St Johns Dr.)
Westminster St. CW2: Crewe 2A 42
Westmorland Ter. CW4: Holm C 3D 28
WESTON .2F 49
Weston Cen. CW1: Crewe 3C 42
Weston Cl. CW9: Nort 2H 15
CW10: Midd 4A 26
Weston Ct. CW2: Shav 2A 48
Weston La. CW2: Basf, Shav 2B 48
Weston Rd. CW1: Crewe 3C 42
CW2: Crewe 5E 43
Westrees CW8: Cudd 2B 12
West Rd. CW8: Weav 4F 7
West St. CW1: Crewe 6G 35
CW1: Hasl 6G 37
CW2: Crewe 6G 35
(not continuous)
CW10: Midd 2A 26
West Vw. CW1: Brad G 1E 35
CW1: Crewe 5H 35
CW9: Nort 5B 10
West Way CW4: Holm C 3D 28
CW11: Sandb 5B 32
Westway CW2: Shav 2B 48
West Wing, The CW10: Bost 4D 20
Westwood Cl. CW2: West 6F 49
Wetton La. CW8: Act B 1C 6
Weycroft M. CW1: Crewe 6A 36
Whalley Rd. CW9: Nort 5A 10
Wharburton Cl. CW8: Sandi 5D 12
Wharf, The CW1: Crewe 1B 42
Wharfdale Av. CW1: Leig 2H 35
WHARTON 1H 23
Wharton Bri. CW7: Wins 5A 20
Wharton (Donefields) Ind. Est.
CW7: Wins 6A 20
Wharton Gdns. CW7: Wins 6A 20
Wharton Hall CW7: Wins 6A 20
Wharton Pk. Rd. CW7: Wins 1H 23
Wharton Retail Pk. CW7: Wins 6H 19
Wharton Rd. CW7: Wins 2H 23
Whatcroft Hall La. CW9: What 1E 21
Wheatfield Cl. CW8: Barn 2C 8
Wheatley Rd. CW1: Crewe 5C 36
Wheelman Rd. CW1: Crewe 4G 35
WHEELOCK 6B 32
Wheelock Cl. CW9: Nort 1H 15
Wheelock Dr. CW7: Wins 2B 24
Wheelock St. CW10: Midd 2A 26
Wheelock Vw. CW10: Midd 4A 26
Whirlow Rd. CW2: Wist 6H 41
Whiston Cl. CW7: Wins 5H 19
Whitby Cl. CW1: Crewe 3H 35
Whitby's La. CW7: Wins 2D 22
White Av. CW2: Crewe 1F 41

Whitebeam Row CW8: Weav 6A 8
(off Walnut Av.)
WHITEGATE 2C 18
Whitegate Cl. CW10: Midd 5A 26
Whitegate Rd. CW7: Wins 5B 18
Whitehall Cl. CW8: Barn 1C 8
Whitehall Dr. CW8: Hart 3E 15
White Hall La. CW11: Warm 1C 30
White Hart Gdns. CW8: Hart 3B 14
White Hart La. CW2: Wist 5E 41
White Horse All. *CW10: Midd* 2A 26
(off Lewin St.)
Whitehouse La. CW5: Nant 1H 45
White Lodge M. CW8: Cudd 4E 13
Whitemore Rd. CW10: Midd 5A 26
White Pk. Cl. CW10: Midd 1B 26
Whites La. CW2: West 1F 49
Whitewell Cl. CW5: Nant 2H 45
Whitley Av. CW8: Barn 2C 8
Whitley Cl. CW10: Midd 4H 25
Whitley Dr. CW8: Hart 3C 14
Whitlow Av. CW5: Nant 3H 45
Whitlow La. CW9: Moul 1H 19
Whittaker Cl. CW1: Crewe 4G 35
Whittington Gdns. CW9: Dave 5H 15
Wickham Ct. CW2: Eng B 4H 49
Wickstead Cl. CW5: Nant 3A 46
Wilbraham Cl. CW5: Act 6C 38
Wilbraham Rd. CW5: Act 6C 38
CW8: Weav 4A 8
Wilderhope Cl. CW2: Wist 6A 42
Wilding St. CW1: Crewe 1C 42
Wilkinson Cl. *CW7: Wins* 5D 22
(off Wilkinson Way)
Wilkinson Way CW7: Wins 4D 22
WILLASTON 1D 46
Willaston Hall Gdns. CW5: Will 1C 46
William Foden Cl. CW11: Elw 2H 31
Williamson Dr. CW5: Nant 2E 45
William St. CW7: Wins 2G 23
CW9: Nort 5B 10
Willowbank CW5: Nant 1H 45
Willow Cl. CW7: Wins 6F 19
Willow Ct. CW5: Nant 6H 39
CW7: Wins 1B 24
CW10: Midd 1A 26
Willow Cres. CW2: Crewe 3F 41
Willow Dr. CW11: Sandb 2G 33
Willow Grn. CW8: Weav 5H 7
Willow Grn. La. CW8: Lit L 1E 7
Willow Gro. CW8: Barn 1D 8
Willows, The CW9: Nort 1G 15
CW9: Winc 6F 5
CW11: Sandb 2D 32
Willows Cl. CW2: Wist 5H 41
Willow Sq. *CW7: Wins* 1A 24
(off Bradbury Rd.)
Wilsbury Grange CW8: Hart 2C 14
Wilson Cres. CW9: L Gral 2H 11
Wilson Dr. CW9: Moul 2H 19
Wilton Cl. CW9: Nort 3G 15
Wincham Av. CW9: Winc 2D 10
Wincham Bus. Pk.
CW9: Winc 2D 10
Wincham La. CW9: Winc 2D 10
Wincham Pk. 3C 10
Winchester Cl. CW2: Shav 4H 47
Winchester Dr. CW2: Eng B 3H 48
(off Abbey Pk. Way)
Windermere Rd. CW2: Crewe 3E 41
CW7: Wins 1E 23
Windings, The CW10: Midd 1H 25
Windsor Av. CW1: Crewe 4G 35
CW5: Nant 4H 45
Windsor Cl. CW8: Cudd 3D 12
Windsor Dr. CW7: Wins 6E 23
Windsor Rd. CW2: Wist 5E 41
Wingfield Pl. CW7: Wins 5D 22
WINNINGTON 4F 9
Winnington Av. CW8: Winn 6D 8
Winnington Hill CW8: Nort 4G 9
Winnington La.
CW8: And, Barn, Nort, Winn 3E 9
Winnington Old La. CW8: Winn 4E 9
Winnington Pk. Recreation Club 4F 9
Winnington St. CW7: Wins 2G 23
CW8: Nort 4H 9

WINSFORD 1F 23
Winsford Cross Shop. Cen.
CW7: Wins 2F 23
Winsford Flash Sailing Club 5H 23
Winsford Ind. Est. CW7: Wins 1C 24
(Road Five)
CW7: Wins 5B 20
(Road One)
Winsford Sports Complex 3F 23
Winsford Station (Rail) 3C 24
Wisdom Wlk. CW11: Elw 2H 31
(off Station Rd.)
WISTASTON 5F 41
Wistaston Av. CW2: Crewe 3F 41
Wistaston Grn. Cl. CW2: Crewe 3E 41
Wistaston Grn. Rd. CW2: Crewe 2C 40
Wistaston Hall 4F 41
Wistaston Pk. CW2: Wist 4F 41
Wistaston Rd. CW2: Crewe 2H 41
CW5: Will 2D 46
Wistaston Rd. Bus. Cen.
CW2: Crewe 1H 41
Wisterdale Cl. CW2: Wist 6G 41
Witham Cl. CW2: Wist 5G 41
Withens Cl. CW8: Weav 5H 7
Withens La. CW8: Weav 5H 7
Withington Cl. CW9: Nort 1A 16
CW11: Sandb 2E 33
Withnall Dr. CW2: Shav 3H 47
Witton Albion FC 3C 10
Witton St. CW9: Nort 4H 9
Witton Wlk. CW9: Nort 5H 9
Woburn Cl. CW9: Nort 2G 15
Wolvesey Pl. CW7: Wins 5D 22
Woodbank Cl. CW2: Wist 6G 41
Woodcott Av. CW7: Wins 2D 22
Woodcott Cl. CW2: Hou 5C 48
Woodend Cl. CW10: Midd 5A 26
Woodford Cl. CW2: Crewe 3F 41
Woodford La. CW7: Wins 3D 22

Woodford La. W. CW7: Wins 4B 22
Woodford Pk. Ind. Est. CW7: Wins 3B 22
Woodham Cl. CW8: Hart 2E 15
Woodland Av. CW1: Crewe 2D 42
CW5: Nant 2H 45
Woodland Gdns. CW1: Crewe 5B 36
Woodlands CW8: Hart 2D 14
Woodlands, The CW8: Winn 5G 9
CW9: Winc 5G 5
Woodlands Dr. CW2: West 4G 49
Woodlands Gro. CW8: Barn 2B 8
Woodlands Rd. CW8: Hart 2D 14
Woodlands Rd. E. CW8: Hart 2E 15
Wood La. CW8: Weav 5A 8
Woodlark Cl. CW7: Wins 3A 24
Woodlea Ct. CW8: Nort 6F 9
Woodnoth Dr. CW2: Shav 2A 48
Woodpecker Dr. CW9: Nort 3H 15
Woodside Av. CW2: Crewe 4F 41
Woodside Dr. CW11: Sandb 3E 33
Woodside La. CW2: Crewe 4F 41
Woodside Ter. CW9: Nort 3B 16
Wood's La. CW8: Crow, Cudd 1A 12
Woodstock Dr. CW10: Midd 6C 26
Wood St. CW2: Crewe 3B 42
Woodward St. CW8: Weav 4H 7
Woolston Dr. CW2: Hou 5C 48
Wordsworth Cl. CW2: Wist 4F 41
CW11: Etti H 3H 31
Wordsworth Dr. CW1: Crewe 1D 42
Works La. CW9: Nort 3E 11
WORLESTON 5A 34
Worleston Cl. CW10: Midd 5A 26
Worsdell Cl. CW2: Crewe 5C 42
Worsdell Ho. CW1: Crewe 1A 42
(off Blount Cl.)
Worthing St. CW9: Nort 5C 10
Worthington Cl. CW5: Nant 2A 46
Wren Av. CW4: Spro 1G 27
Wrenbury Dr. CW9: Nort 2G 15

Wrenmere Cl. CW11: Sandb 1A 32
Wrexham Rd. CW5: Burl 6A 38
Wright Av. CW9: Rudh 1C 16
Wright Ct. CW5: Nant 2H 45
Wrights La. CW11: Sandb 3F 33
WYBUNBURY 6G 47
Wybunbury La. CW5: Stap, Wyb 4B 46
Wybunbury Moss (National Nature Reserve)
. . . . .6H 47
Wybunbury Rd. CW5: Will 2D 46
Wyche Av. CW5: Nant 2F 45
Wyche Cl. CW9: Rudh 1E 17
Wyche Ho. Bank CW5: Nant 2F 45
Wych-House La. CW10: Midd 2A 26
Wychwood Pk. CW2: West 5F 49
Wyncroft Ct. CW8: Weav 4G 7
(off Smith's La.)
Wyndham Cl. CW9: Nort 2H 15

Y

Yarwood Cl. CW8: Nort 6H 9
Yatehouse La. CW10: Byl 4H 21
Yates St. CW2: Crewe 3A 42
Yewlands CW8: Cudd 2B 12
Yew Tree Cl. CW10: Midd 1H 25
Yew Tree Dr. CW5: Nant 2F 45
CW8: Barn 1D 8
Yew Tree Rd. CW2: Wist 5G 41
York Dr. CW7: Wins 5F 23

Z

Zan Dr. CW11: Whee 6C 32
Zan Ind. Pk. CW11: Whee 6C 32
Zion St. CW8: Nort 6G 9

The representation on the maps of a road, track or footpath is no evidence of the existence of a right of way.

The Grid on this map is the National Grid taken from Ordnance Survey® mapping with the permission of the Controller of Her Majesty's Stationery Office.

SAFETY CAMERA INFORMATION

Safety camera locations are publicised by the Safer Roads Partnership who operate them in order to encourage drivers to comply with speed limits at these sites. It is the driver's absolute responsibility to be aware of and to adhere to speed limits at all times.

By showing this safety camera information it is the intention of Geographers' A-Z Map Company Ltd., to encourage safe driving and greater awareness of speed limits and vehicle speed. Data accurate at time of printing.

Printed and bound in the United Kingdom by Gemini Press Ltd., Shoreham-by-Sea, West Sussex
Printed on materials from a sustainable source